Unlock the Genius Within

Neurobiological Trauma, Teaching, and Transformative Learning

Daniel S. Janik

Rowman & Littlefield Education
Lanham, Maryland • Toronto • Oxford
2005

Published in the United States of America
by Rowman & Littlefield Education
A Division of Rowman & Littlefield Publishers, Inc.
A wholly owned subsidary of The Rowman & Littlefield Publishing Group, Inc.
4501 Forbes Boulevard, Suite 200, Lanham, Maryland 20706
www.rowmaneducation.com

PO Box 317
Oxford
OX2 9RU, UK

British Library Cataloguing in Publication Information Available

Library of Congress Cataloging-in-Publication Data

Janik, Daniel S.
  Unlock the genius within : neurobiological trauma, teaching, and
transformative learning / Daniel S. Janik.
      p. cm.
  Includes bibliographical references and index.
  ISBN 1-57886-291-4 (pbk. : alk. paper)
  1. Learning—Physiological aspects. 2. Teaching. 3. Neurobiology. I. Title.
  LB1057.J36 2005
  370.15'23—dc22   2005006066

Contents

Preface
Chance Encounters

After twenty-five years of medical practice, research, and teaching, I decided to pursue another related professional interest of mine: education, or how humans acquire language and knowledge—ultimately, how we learn.

This book is in large part a surprising look back for me at what at first seemed a remarkable set of chance developments in my medical career. Clearly, over the years my practice had become increasingly focused on language as I began to deal more and more with some of the most vulnerable of patients—those who had been traumatically injured by a blow, shock, or unusual stress. My first patients were newborns whose lives were tied to a newborn intensive care unit. Following them and my other patients from infancy through childhood, adolescence, and young adulthood, I began to notice the powerful effect of those traumatic events on their physical as well as psychological lives. But what specifically caught my attention was that these effects seemed to be associated with not just one but many different kinds of trauma that occur throughout life.

I wasn't looking for a breakthrough in learning at that time. I was a traditionally trained preventive medicine and public health practitioner. Many of my own beliefs about how to help trauma patients—and later ultimately all learners—were dramatically altered by what I am going to share in this book. Nor did the breakthrough occur suddenly, in a sudden flash of understanding. It occurred slowly and steadily, and followed what was then a strange and surprising path from trauma to effective, nontraumatic learning.

But for the moment, please return with me to my practice involving patients recovering from trauma: One of the first shocks to my own belief system was the almost overwhelming number of traumatic injuries people

suffer, and suffer silently, in this world. While the public focuses on infa-
mously spectacular events, trauma actually appears many times throughout the lives of most people. These traumas, sometimes lasting only a few
seconds, are commonly ignored or forgotten—technically repressed.

In fact, trauma in the strictest sense can occur as a result of any number
of unwanted events, not necessarily originating outside of one's self. Most
would agree that the severity of the trauma is most important, but over
time I came to realize that the sense of loss of control is another, even
more significant factor in determining the depth and severity of the
trauma. By its very nature, trauma is not just physical violation; it is an
unwanted violation of power over one's body, mind, and spirit.

Once I began to study the effects of trauma in this manner, I became increasingly impressed that even trauma of the briefest duration constitutes
a major learning event. Traumatically learned lessons, even when the
trauma is later forgotten or repressed, seem to cause persistent changes in
behavior throughout life. During the last ten years, I became especially
impressed with the effectiveness of learning associated with trauma and
wondered if the processes involved in traumatic learning and, of course,
recovery might offer insights into learning in general.

At the same time, I became more and more impressed with the importance to trauma survivors of communicating to others their experience of an
event so extraordinary that it overwhelmed not only their mind, body, and
spirit, but in fact their very communicative ability, and thereby their linguistic resources. I observed with awe the sheer immensity of this struggle
during psychotherapy (oral expression); reading, documenting, and journal-
ing; art therapy (creative and symbolic expression as well as interpretation),
music therapy (aural, tonal, rhythmic, and guttural expression), massage
therapy (tactile reception and expression), partial and whole body movement therapy, sexual therapy, social therapy, even occupational therapy—all
directed at "speaking the unspeakable." In essence, they were acquiring a
new (technically a second or, more appropriately, subsequent) "language"
replete with new vocabulary (grammatical), communicative structures, and
discourse strategies, the purpose of which was to convey, rethink, and ultimately try to "re-solve" the trauma. This challenge seemed common to virtually every survivor I saw who desired some form of recovery.

Even more importantly, I noticed that during that process it was possible for survivors to self-modify portions of what they had so effectively

learned traumatically, and my awakened interest in subsequent language acquisition and learning became a passion. Was it possible that what I was observing in these special cases was in fact not only the key to a new understanding of language acquisition, but also a form of effective, non-traumatic learning?

My interest in the field of language acquisition and learning led me back to a time over 20 centuries ago—to Greece, when a young student, Plato, watched helplessly as his mentor and master, Socrates, was sentenced to death for his teachings by his own people. Plato described and later published his firsthand account of Socrates' trial, condemnation, and eventual suicide. What resulted from this horrific trauma was the establishment of a second school of teaching and thought (what Plato called philosophy). He turned away from the Socratic path to knowledge, rooted in sensory-based self-discovery, and created his own Platonic path to knowledge, based on the teaching of "ideals"—pure ideas that were perfect representations of our imperfect, physical world—that a living master could grasp and pass along. This second, safer path eventually led to the establishment of schools, as well as the concept of fees for professional teaching services, both cornerstones of modern teaching. Over the centuries, Socratic learning yielded to Platonic teaching, until even the existence of Socratic learning, not withstanding our current ideational concept of "critical thinking," became largely ignored and in increasing instances forgotten altogether.

It wasn't until the eighteenth century that the physicians Gall (1758–1828), Bouillard (1796–1881), Broca (1824–1880), Wernicke (1848–1905), Jackson (1834–1911), Kussmaul (1822–1902), and Freud (1856–1939) were able to join forces with such educational luminaries as von Humboldt (1767–1835), Schleicher (1821–1868), Muller (1823–1900), Steinthal (1823–1899), Steiner (1861–1925), and Lenneberg (1921–1975) to create a "new" German school of learning, loosely called "biomedical linguistics," based on explaining how language is learned using biological and medical, rather than philosophical, social and ideational information—that the possibility of unifying these two philosophies (Socratic and Platonic) became once again a possibility—a long time to recover from a single trauma!

It seemed to me from my new physician-turned-psychologist-turned-educator-turned-linguist point of view that these two classical philosophies were destined to intersect. My own clinical observations on traumatic learning helped me build on the German school of thought and formulate what I have only recently come to realize is nothing short of an entirely new understanding of learning—a theory and method of learning based on the fundamental neural and biological processes involved in learning. I call this theory and method neurobiological learning.

Ever the skeptic, I was nonetheless held in check by two nagging concerns: First, the value of any new theory must always be examined, measured, and evaluated in terms of the richness of its explanatory power. Just adding another new theory to an already long list of new, fashionable theories and methods of teaching and learning could actually prove counterproductive. Second, I wanted to present not just a new theory, but one complete with method, testable hypotheses, and tenets (fundamental laws)—a theory robust enough to actually change, consolidate, and advance the long list of current theories and methods, and create the potential for discovery of new knowledge and wisdom.

In 1999 I was invited by Joel Weaver, director of the Intercultural Communications College in Honolulu, Hawaii, and the school's owners to critically examine and, if possible, revitalize a failing English as a second language course in American Academic English. I immediately agreed to take the job if, with his permission, I could apply my emerging neurobiological theory and method. What resulted was an extraordinary learning event, replete with extraordinary, often counterintuitive discoveries about learning that, as I had hoped, went far beyond the particular course, and even beyond learning English as a subsequent or even first language. It went the whole way: to how we learn almost anything effectively!

Having satisfied my initial concerns about the effectiveness of the theory and method in the classroom, I am pleased to present a complete theory and method, along with some most extraordinary findings—tenets— as well as some testable hypotheses (predictions). First, I need to present some of the medical and clinical observations that led me to this new theory of learning, and the important biological and medical information from which it was born.

Whenever and wherever possible, I have eliminated or replaced as much of the medical, biological, linguistic, and educational jargon as possible, though at times, when there is simply no way around the precision of a particular tongue-twisting construct, I have tried to accompany it with a nontechnical explanation. If, on the other hand, any of my explanations seem less than technically satisfying, or you find that you would like to delve more deeply into the details of neurobiological learning, I invite you to read my academic book *A Neurobiological Theory and Method of Language Acquisition*, aimed at university teachers, educators, linguists, physicians, psychologists, and neurobiologists.

Given the breakneck speed with which we are unraveling the innermost workings of the human body and mind, it's no exaggeration to say that neurobiological learning goes far beyond language acquisition, linguistics, and even education. I believe that the foundations of neurobiological learning described in this book will eventually provide a kind of genetic map of the fundamental geography of learning itself.

Acknowledgments

In 2004, when my doctoral dissertation, *A Neurobiological Theory and Method of Language Acquisition,* was finally published, I had no idea of the interest and impact it would have *outside* the cloistered halls of academia. In less than six months, what was envisioned to be a limited run of a highly technical explanation of neurobiological learning theory and methodology in language acquisition entered its third printing, and—happily—demand for it continued to increase! I am thankful to the many dedicated readers willing to wade through the immense and often difficult jargon . . . and those who wrote me with comments, experiences, and support. These are dedicated readers! Thank you!

But I wanted you to know that *I heard you*! Many of you requested I write another book—one stripped of jargon—that was friendlier, in which I could talk more directly to you, highlighting the most compelling and important contemporary contributions to neurobiological learning (NL) in general, and tell more about application of its nontraumatic derivative, transformational learning, at the Intercultural Communications College (ICC) in Honolulu, Hawaii, where I first introduced it into the classroom. That's what this second book is about: It's for you—interested educators, teachers, tutors, mentors, students, learners, and parents of learners—who want to know more about NL and an alternative to traumatic learning, that of transformational learning (TL).

I searched hard to find a professional writer with whom I could collaborate on this project. There were so many interested, outstanding professional writers, as well as area and topic professionals, leaders in education and learning, and even parents with a personal interest in seeing TL implemented at their particular school to help their children. But it was in

Jack Howard that I finally found them all, and it is to Jack that I offer my sincerest thanks for his unflagging efforts to get both neurobiological and transformational learning into the hands of the most important learners and advocates—you! Thank you, Jack!

While not as evident, I would like to acknowledge the contributions of Margaret Bills, the first "successful" NL mentor-candidate at ICC to "get it all." Without our many and varied hallway consultations between classes, this book would not have been complete. Maggie, by the way, has been working for several years with me to redesign two of ICC's central NL learning resources: the *TOEFL 2 Student Study Guide*, and a mentor's resource guide—all while completing a master's degree. And there's also my dual-mastered colleague, Christina Widjaja, an outstanding, classically trained teacher of English as a second language who, for over two years now, has faithfully served as our teacher "control." Thank you, Maggie and Christina. No researcher or author could ask for more in terms of support and dedication from colleagues.

A recent addition to our NL/TL group, Hisako Saito, a former student of mine who actually experienced the application of neurobiological/transformational learning theory and methodology as an English as a second language student in the ICC classroom, subsequently went on to complete a master's degree in teaching English as a second language at the University of Hawaii at Manoa. She has kindly spent many hours reviewing my first book and particularly this one for correctness from both a technical and experiential point of view. Hisako is currently reexamining *TOEFL by Internet*, our distance-learning, subsequent language acquisition program, to more incorporate the newest derivative of neurobiological learning, disquisitional learning (DL). I am deeply honored that a neurobiological learner should subsequently consider dedicating a lifetime to the study and pursuit of NL, TL, DL, and beyond!

More transparent, but no less important, have been the continual inspiration and frequent critical analyses offered by both ICC's academic director, Chris Guro, and its overall director, Mr. Joel Weaver, whose command of subsequent language acquisition theory and methodology have proven time and again to be absolutely invaluable. Thanks, Chris and Joel, for keeping me honest!

I recently had the pleasure of presenting NL theory and methodology before the combined English Language Teaching and Learning faculty and students of Brigham Young University (BYU), Laie (Hawaii). As a result, Dr. Lynne Hansen, professor of applied linguistics, kindly agreed to critically review this manuscript. Dr. Hansen's comments and suggestions, both written and during subsequent discussions, proved invaluable in helping me clarify some of the "stickier" points of NL/TL in a nontechnical way.

Heartfelt thanks to reviewers Judy Ireton, Ted Ireton, Arthur Wallace, and Ruth Janik for previewing this book and providing comments, suggestions, and advice. Finally, my special thanks and my eternal loving gratitude to my dear life partner, Setsuko Tsuchiya, a natural healer whose dedication to education and undying belief in the learning and healing power of movement therapy provided a lifeline during my own darkest moments of prediscovery frustration and doubt.

A quick word about the "subjects" I described in my previous book, some of whom have their place in this one as well. Yes, they represent actual survivors I have known and had the privilege of working with over the years. I have, however, taken the liberty of changing their names (and thereby their initials) and in several instances have presented similar cases as a composite single. I hope you will forgive me. Without their individual and collective experience, this book would not have been conceived. Yet it is of absolute importance that I protect and defend their identities.

Writing a nontechnical book about a new, biophysically based subject like NL and TL presented some unresolvable challenges. I am certain that some readers will find this book a welcome relief—a fast and easy way to discover NL and TL without the jargon getting in the way. I hope so. I realize at the same time that some others may find the explanations and examples in this book too conversational or anecdotal, less than complete or satisfying, and perhaps on occasion even irritatingly homespun in style. To these readers I commend my original academic work, with its over 250 technical references from contemporary academic books and professional journals.

My first book was a labor of the mind, born in travail. This second book is a labor of love. It is through love and, in the "new" tradition of transformational learning, unassuming kindness, and curiosity, that what has been successfully born will continue to develop, mature, and endure. It is within the nurturing arms of Jack, Maggie, Hisako, Christina, Chris, Joel,

Lynne, readers like you, and many physicians, researchers, educators, teachers, tutors, students, learners, and parents that neurobiological and transformational learning now enters its childhood. It is my sincerest wish that this new kind of learning will challenge and ultimately change the learning world forever. God knows, we need it!

Introduction

If you stop to think of it, while we often hear, read, and, especially if you're a parent, end up heatedly debating how well (or badly) our schools teach English, science, math, computing, the arts, and even physical education, there is very little said about the more important, underlying issue: how well we learn.

Notice that I didn't say the way we teach. Everyone seems to argue continually about teachers, class sizes, or what should be taught, but very few acknowledge the necessary, revolutionary task of defining and eventually implementing effective learning. Perhaps it's because the question, on reflection, cuts so deeply into our individual and personal, rather than our tougher collective, social psyche. Yet it is the question "How do we learn?" that I believe is at the heart of contemporary school and teaching problems. The noted educator C. P. Snow, in his controversial book *The Two Cultures*, noted that whether "one begins by thinking only of the intellectual life, or only of the social life, one comes to a point where it becomes manifest that our education has gone wrong, and gone wrong in the same way" (Snow 1998, p. 33–34).

I ended up coming to the same radical conclusion while working as an English as a second language instructor at the Intercultural Communications College. This is significant: It was a surprise for me to observe how stressful, even sometimes traumatic, learning a subsequent language was for so many "normal" students. Given this, the power of traumatic learning, and the extent to which it interferes with our daily lives, understanding how traumatic learning works and affects us in the classroom should be of great interest to all teachers, including our ultimate teachers: parents. Yet how many parents, classroom teachers, and educators do you know who truly understand how the mind actually learns in the absence of, during, or after trauma? Not many, I would guess. Even one?

In fact, most of the teachers I work with, whether at small private language schools or large public universities, are well trained in classical Platonic-style teaching but know little about Socratic-style learning, traumatic learning, or the neurobiology of learning. That is to say that they had been amply trained in the "business of education," but not in how individual students actually acquire what they, the teachers, try to teach them. In some instances I have been impressed with how much can be learned despite the constantly changing teaching methods and styles being applied: Learning in spite of teaching! Of course it is easy to make broad generalizations like these. But what it boils down to is that what I was looking for was the same thing that interested teachers needed to know: a way to uncover the connection, if any, between Platonic-style teaching and the largely forgotten Socratic-style of learning. To do this, I knew, would require an "eyes wide open" journey, this time as an educator, back into the mythical world of the early Greek philosophers and the dark world of traumatic learning where I had worked earlier as a physician. So now it is time to invite you to begin accompanying me "back to the future," to what I consider one of the more interesting, well-published, and yet little-known experiments in traumatic learning.

Most knowledgeable trauma specialists will agree that one of the best-chronicled examples of traumatic learning came from the early 1900s, under circumstances impossible to replicate today—an experiment involving the deliberate traumatization of a nine-month-old child named Albert B. The researchers, John Watson and Rosalie Rayner, in a daring series of experiments published under the title "Conditioned Emotional Reactions" in the *Journal of Experimental Psychology* in 1920, comment about their test subject: "his stability was one of the principal reasons for using him as a subject in this test. We felt that we could do him relatively little harm . . ." (p. 1).

Albert B. was indeed a special case and seemed to present a special challenge: According to Watson and Rayner, "No one had ever seen him in a state of fear and rage. The infant practically never cried" (p. 2).

They therefore suspended, next to the child, a four-foot-long steel bar that made a frighteningly loud noise (the trauma) when struck with a metal hammer. On only the third blow, they met with success, producing for the first time a fearful response in Albert to the point of crying.

Albert was then shown a white rat at the same time the trauma was repeated. Albert quickly began to connect the rat with the trauma; when shown the white rat alone, he would immediately begin crying. Soon, when he was shown a white rabbit without any accompanying noise, he would begin to cry, having associated small, white, furry animals with trauma. Eventually, Albert would be shown to react negatively to dogs, white cotton, and even a furry seal coat.

I think you would agree with me that this appalling experiment should not be duplicated. And yet it's funny (in a darkly humorous way) how many times and ways it *is* repeated, isn't it? This single account is actually quite enough to demonstrate the incredible power of traumatic learning. First, it can link a feeling (for example, Albert's fear) or a response (Albert's crying) with both the trauma and any of a wide range of objects introduced at the same time (in this case, a white rat—technically, a principal or central learning object). What makes an object principal or central is that it is introduced in the center of the learner's attention. Second, it can link a feeling or a response to a wide range of other objects that just happen to also be present—a bright light or a particular smell, for example— that the learner isn't even aware of. In such a case, a bright light, like sunshine, or a particular smell, like cigarette smoke—technically speaking, a "peripheral learning object"—can accidentally become linked to the central object, the response, and/or the trauma. Third, the link can transfer to other objects that in some way seem similar to the learner—for example, when Albert started becoming afraid of dogs. Virtually any kind of similarity is enough to make the link. The important point here is that what is learned traumatically is not only powerful, but widely transferable. It can be introduced intentionally (as in traumatic teaching) or occur accidentally at any time. It can transfer not only to things that we are aware of, but also to things we are not aware of.

What quickly became clear to me in my practice was that linkage was also true in reverse: secondary objects—things we aren't aware of—can trigger not only traumatic feelings like anxiety or fear, and responses like crying or suddenly becoming tense and silent, but trauma itself. That is, trauma can not only reinforce itself, but even create new trauma—complete with additional learned feelings and responses—often outside our aware-ness. Traumatic learning is indeed powerful and effective. And let's not for-get at this point what trauma is: Trauma is any unwanted violation of one's body, mind, and/or spirit.

While experimenters today continue to investigate the nature of trau-matic learning and its side effects, for example, on laboratory rats rather than six-month-old infants, there are literally millions of "test subjects" walking around outside the laboratory every day—the so-called "walking wounded"—who have suffered the myriad traumas of daily life. And while they may have "forgotten" the original trauma, central objects, feel-ings, or responses, they still react just as quickly and strongly as Albert, in a vast and complex mess of learned ways to anything that somehow re-minds them of it. But I would like to return for a moment to central learn-ing objects (Albert B.'s white rat) and trauma.

A number of years ago, I was having a late lunch at a favorite local restaurant. With me was a young man consulting with me about the pos-sibility of needing some professional counseling. We were both startled by a loud noise, probably a car backfiring, from the street outside. Almost in-stantaneously, certainly before I could react or comment, my companion was crouching under the table. If you had been sitting with us, you prob-ably would have regarded this kind of behavior as atypical, unusual, or maybe even seriously abnormal. But his response was not in and of itself inappropriate—if you knew the circumstances of the original trauma (in this case, a particularly intense moment during a battle in Vietnam).

The "problem" in this case is the context within which this particular traumatically learned response occurred. In a battle, where a loud bang would likely be accompanied by bullets flying everywhere, my lack of re-sponse would have been abnormal and probably life-threatening. That is, my lunch partner's response was entirely appropriate for another place and time, and possibly also even in the future. After this incident I thought about how traumatic learning helps us acquire a set of essential survival reflexes. There would be little point if essential survival reflexes were lost as quickly and easily as they are acquired. By the way, at a later discus-sion, my lunch companion mentioned that he did not recall hearing the loud noise when it occurred, and almost instantly "forgot" the whole episode, much like with the original trauma, until I specifically asked him about it.

Another absolutely amazing aspect of traumatic learning is that it is just as effective whether the violation of power is directly experienced or "just" observed. In fact, I have noticed again and again in my practice that a powerless observer can be even more deeply affected than the person who was the direct target of the violation.

When looked at in this way, traumatic learning opportunities occur more than every day. Just read the newspapers or watch a good "action" movie. Violence—trauma—is always right there "in your face," whether you see it (centrally) or not (peripherally). The sheer number of potential traumatic learning events collectively suggests that effective teaching (or learning, depending on your perspective) is probably not as simple, well defined, or well understood as it might at first appear. This is, interestingly, true of teaching theories in general: A recent search of the linguistic literature revealed, for example, at least 40 different teaching "theories" associated with language acquisition alone. Of course, counting theories isn't what this is all about. What I needed to find was whether all these theories had something in common, and if they did, whether it was in fact somehow related to trauma.

At face value, most contemporary teaching theories and methodologies do not appear to have a lot in common, and certainly little, if any, basis in trauma. Even so, I decided to carefully relook at them with regard to some commonly discussed elements: their *style* (reason, logic, and proof); the *source material* from which they are derived; the formative *approaches* utilized in their development; and the informational *resources* upon which they are based. And this began a series of startling discoveries . . .

Chapter One

Yet *Another* Teaching Theory

THE TIES THAT BIND

Most current teaching theories and methodologies are proven (in technical terms, validated) by building directly on what everyone agrees is generally true—commonly, what authorities in the field believe and say. It's the same way we hope the news is being reliably reported in a newspaper. This style, technically "direct logic," is the intellectual mainstay of modern academic, literary, social, and in some instances even psychological inquiry. By its nature, this style of proof assumes the reliability of common sense and authoritative ideas, such as for example the grass growing faster in spring than in winter. These so-called "scholarly" or "rhetorical" proofs have rooted within them the power of common sense and authoritative knowledge. Unfortunately, they do not always result in "true" theories or hypotheses. In fact, most are more in the nature of a new or interesting idea, and others simply reflect the newest intellectual fad or popular saying.

Rhetorical proofs, in the narrow sense, support a single opinion or point—a thesis if you will—and a set of supporting arguments, which are often mistaken for a theory and hypotheses. While theses may look, sound, smell, and feel like theories, they are not. Theories must, in the end, be indirectly proven using physical data; classical rhetorical, educational, and linguistic theses, on the other hand, are derived directly from authoritative ideas and examples. For example, grammar-translation, psycholinguistic, and sociolinguistic "theories" of language teaching and their attendant arguments and methodologies rarely, if ever, draw on human anatomical, physiological, or biochemical data. In fact, their seeming "power" comes from the very fact that they are independent of physical data. They seem to work, no matter what the situation. But direct proofs are only as strong as the extent to which the information on which they are built is "true"—that is, relates to each and every physical application. Indirect proofs, the sine qua non of scientific inquiry, by their very nature challenge the truth and appropriateness of each information item as it actually relates to the physical world and specific situation. In other words, theories are grounded in physical data experienced Socratic-style by our senses, whereas theses are based on ideas and Platonic ideals.

To illustrate, consider for a moment the question "How does a car work?" The process by which a car works is, like teaching, neither as simplistic nor entirely well understood, at least by most of us, as it might first appear. An investigation into the nature of cars could be handled in a variety of different ways. For example, one could carefully examine the meaning of "car"—what linguists call a "semantic" approach. On the other hand, one could examine the noises that cars (and for that matter, their drivers) make, and create a look-up grammar-translator of "car talk." One could, on the other hand, focus on operational cues—the various signs, signals, and devices that tell us what to do next—a more "discourse"-oriented approach. One could also study the particular ways that American cars and drivers, through sounds, patterns, rhythms, dialects (for example, cursing), and inflections attempt to communicate in a broadly "audiolingual" or "communicative" style. Or, one could investigate the psychological or social relevance of cars, "psycho-socio-linguistically" speaking. One could even analyze cars in terms of computational switch and flow diagrams, logic circuitry, or other forms of artificial intelligence. Or, you could just believe that cars are self-designed: "Just built that way." You could just as well believe that cars grow on trees.

From any of these perspectives, each purposefully reminiscent of one or more current scholarly "theories," a resulting research effort might go something like this: Cars move. That obviously requires power. A car's power is often expressed in terms of horsepower. If cars are powered by horsepower, then what color is the horse?

I admit that this is absurd. Yet that's the point! This kind of research is not all that different from that behind many of today's contemporary academic educational "theories." In 1934 the Russian psychologist I. P. Pavlov, at one of his famous "Wednesday" lectures, summed it up this way: "How can anyone get to know the whole without breaking it up? Take, for example, the simplest machine. How can the principle of its working be understood, if it is not dismantled, if the interdependence of its [physical] parts is not considered?" (p. 572)

Most linguistic and educational theories in vogue today are rhetorical and ideational, and at best recusant. In less fancy jargon, this is akin to teaching someone to drive without explaining anything about how a car physically works. It's OK as long as everything works perfectly during the demonstration drive, but it's not at all OK when, after driving it off the new car lot, the first little thing goes wrong. Worse, this kind of teaching short shrifts not only the current learner, but also the next generation of learners and teachers, who eventually forget what a car even is or, to return to our topic, how a learner actually learns. Ironically, this loss also involves considerable wasted effort, as it gets in the way of both critical thinking and the acquisition of knowledge. What is "learned" in this manner must now be unlearned before it can be relearned properly. Sadly, this isn't a new or unusual situation in teaching; it's been going on since Plato. Many of the trappings of modern classroom teaching—ideas about schools and classrooms, the emphasis on the importance of academic authority, and even the direct style of proof—can be traced back to the forced suicide of Plato's mentor, clearly an unprecedented example of effective traumatic learning! Ironically, it was from Plato's pupil, Aristotle, that the indirect method of inquiry and proof using physical data spread.

I have already mentioned that a rich biolinguistic tradition began to flower in what I call the new German school during the nineteenth and twentieth centuries, laying the necessary foundation for a possible return to Socratic learning traditions at the same time that our neurobiological understanding of how the mind actually works began to develop. Physicians, scientists, and linguists all began looking at the same information, though some, even now, continue to look at the data through rose-colored Platonic glasses rather than microscopes. Kathie Sarachild, one of the early originators and staunch supporters of "consciousness raising," correctly summarized this "nexus rising" in the simplest of terms: "Study nature, not books."

Good theories and methods do more than present us with reflections of the latest ideas and fads, and "talk the talk." They must be street smart and also reflect the world as it physically exists. This obviously has a lot to do with the kinds of data and information involved and the sources of that data and information.

INTO THE LAIR

Let us consider, for a moment, the psycholinguistic approach ('psycho" or "psyche" referring to the mind, and "linguistic" to language: "mind language"). Psycholinguistics is both a contemporary theory and a method that draws heavily upon human psychology to explain language in all its facets, including acquisition, listening, speaking, reading, and writing. Behaviors like these are where all psychologically related theories are eventually road-tested. Modern psycholinguistics is forever indebted to Sigmund Freud for his ideas on the psychopathology ('psycho" alludes to mind, and pathology, its problems) of the human mind. At its best, an impressive array of behavioral tools is available to the psycholinguist. At its worst, psycholinguistics, by its historical reliance on direct, authoritative proofs of ideas, can quickly and easily change a physical reality, like clinical depression, into a shadow captured in a mirror-in-mirror Wonderland, like an unbalanced id or superego, and back. Convenient. And tricky.

Admittedly, as a clinical physician I frequently use—and even rely on—Freudian theses in my practice. However, I don't use them because they are particularly efficient or effective, or because they advance my knowledge of the physical workings of my patients' minds. Quite frankly, I use them, like most contemporary linguistic and educational theses, because there's simply nothing better immediately available. If I needed water and I knew someone who had found some using a dousing stick, I'd accept the water, no matter how it was found. The problem with "rhetorical teaching theories" is that they are not theories at all—they depend primarily on authority, a lot of trust, and a touch of luck or magic.

Even now, I have to constantly remind myself whenever I reach for a psycholinguistic justification that, as with Freud's concepts of "id," "ego," and "superego," what I will end up with are really ideational justifications—rationalizations—and intellectualizations—old fads—that quite simply are not grounded in physical data. The noted philosopher Ludwig Wittgenstein, a contemporary of Freud, says it ever so much more colorfully: "Freud's fanciful pseudo explanations (precisely because they are so brilliant) perform a disservice. Now any ass has these pictures to use in 'explaining' symptoms of illness" (p. 49).

But there's more. Modern teaching theses and methods focus on similarities—generalities—and ignore difficult-to-rationalize "natural" exceptions to human learning, like traumatic learning, which is often "explained" as "counterintuitive." Perhaps. But all humans have suffered trauma to some extent. All of us are subject to the effects of both conscious and unconscious, or forgotten, traumatic learning. It would be hoped that most teachers would enter their profession aware of their wounds, blindness, and unconscious attempts to control that have resulted from unexamined experiences with trauma. This would impact the selection of theses, theories, approaches, and methodologies selected or ignored in the classroom. If this sounds preposterous (and it admittedly sounds so even as I write it), consider that humans, simply by virtue of being born, routinely suffer from a significant, collective natal trauma and amnesia that blinds us from the very beginning to the fundamental learning processes that eventually shape much of our entire existence. Plato credits Socrates as saying that most of us spend our entire lives attempting to recover what we knew but lost at birth.

THE BEST LAID SCHEMES O' MICE AN' MEN

Teaching requires teachers to focus almost exclusively on usual—normative—classroom information. Yet if there is one painful lesson that I have learned from my years in clinical medicine and science, it's that the "Big Picture" is rarely visible from the study of normative information. Most advances in human understanding have come from examination and explanation, not of stacks of normative information, but from the exception—the one that doesn't fit. If a real educational theory could be constructed from what we know clinically about traumatic learning (an exceptional, particularly effective form of learning), then the result should be fundamentally different from the many theses based on normative classroom information. This is the case with neurobiological theory.

Ultimately, the theory and the resulting method should explain both the exceptional and the normative physical data based on how brains and minds actually work. It should provide immediate, new insights into how traumatic and nontraumatic learning works within a learner's brain. When applied to nontraumatic situations, the results should be just as effective as with traumatic learning, and maybe even more so. This is, of course, easier said than done. It's been many years since Socrates walked the earth, and despite the *physical* evidence supporting Socratic inquiry and its effectiveness when applied in almost any situation, normative or non-normative, most educated people cling to Platonism or some variant of it.

But it's not just a matter of effectiveness. Consider for a moment the different results of their application: The differences between Socratic and Platonic knowledge, for example, are much deeper than just personal preference. It is the very difficulty of unlearning unwanted information and knowledge that does not fit into our physical, neurosensory world—all the "nonsense" ideational information and knowledge gained from Platonic-taught traumatic learning—that ultimately disadvantages Platonic-based teaching.

TOOLS OF THE TRADE

Most linguistic and educational theses are, as I mentioned, based on teaching studies restricted to an artificial environment called the "classroom." In reality, learning and education occur and progress not so much in school, but in the laboratory of life.

My clinical research began at the proverbial beginning of that "reality" laboratory—in pediatric neonatal intensive care units (NICUs), treating traumatized newborns. At that time, in early to mid-1970, many of my medical colleagues held that premature newborns, like fetuses, were not neurobiologically mature enough to experience pain, and were thereby not subject to trauma during NICU treatment or its consequences. Perhaps this was a necessary belief, given the aggressive, invasive nature of the many treatments. "Routine" three- or four-hour arterial punctures for blood gases, for example, are quite traumatic in both the literal and learning sense. The positive side of the NICU was that, for some of us, it focused attention on these traumas and, when recognized as such, on what we were traumatically teaching these newborns, and placed the two close enough together for us to begin connecting them. The goal of neonatal intensive care has always been aggressive treatment, rapid stabilization of the patient, and ultimately getting them out of the intensive care environment as quickly as possible, making it a highly complex environment for studying traumatic learning.

I also provided long-term follow-up care to NICU survivors. The care in this situation was less aggressive and invasive, but hardly nontraumatic. I had more time to observe, and the question of inherited versus learned behavior, nature versus nurture, arose. Childhood is a formative period that should create a well-adjusted, stable individual, able to function reasonably well throughout life. Most of us, however, have seen "normal" children with one or more alcoholic parents, or who were raised in a dysfunctional or abusive family. Some of these "normal" kids become the classroom agitators and disruptors of tomorrow, bullying other children in and out of schoolrooms, and seemingly going out of their way to make the lives of others miserable. Others go to the other extreme and become exceptional achievers. Still others become so quiet they seem to blend into the very walls and disappear.

My clinical impression was that the physical results of early trauma, which physicians traditionally focus on, were actually small in comparison to the late psychological effects. Survivors "learned about learning" as the result of the trauma, and seemed destined to carry traumatic learning with them throughout life. In the problems I awakened to and began looking for, I found uniformly that depression, anxiety, and dyslexia were expected, given the extent of the trauma, and became apparent. But it was things like unusual phobias (fears of nonthreatening objects like in one example, spoons, and another, apples), panic attacks, chronic tiredness, and a variety of behavioral quirks—the echoes of traumatic injury that my luncheon guest experienced—that most intrigued me and, at last, firmly captured my interest.

For most of these survivors, the traumatic event was, given their state of psychological development at that time, so extraordinary that it had entirely overwhelmed their ability to understand what was happening. This probably doesn't seem so surprising today, with our better understanding of trauma and its effects. But back in 1970, it was considered by many to be totally radical.

Radical or not, I kept noting that many survivors had great trouble "speaking the unspeakable" to those of us who hadn't suffered their particular traumatic circumstances. It was in these outpatient clinics that I

began to find a link—a common thread—between these two vastly different worlds. If survivors could somehow learn how to speak what was unspeakable, it might be possible, given their greater neurobiological maturity and wider experience, to "unlearn" some of what was unwanted and
yet so effectively learned. Perhaps they could even *effectively relearn*
everything from a new point of view, one that would afford them more behavioral choices and flexibility. I began to wonder if there was a way I
could help them ultimately communicate what they experienced, so they
could let go of the need to spend so much energy repressing the trauma,
and redirect that energy into healing.

My work eventually expanded to include adults struggling with psychological recovery from a wide variety of traumas, for example, physical battery, sexual violation, and natural disasters. My interests, however,
continued to focus quite narrowly on how survivors in general went about
acquiring a subsequent language and the communication ability that
would allow them to describe, convey, and eventually resolve what they
had learned traumatically.

Later, when I formally shifted from medicine to linguistics, I began to
appreciate the depth of this problem and the unique contributions made by
the enlightened linguists and educators of the German school. My own individual knowledge of medicine, biology, education, and now linguistics
was individually inadequate. But combined, they provided the breadth
necessary to begin to ferret out the nature of effective learning—the
"missing link," or informational bridge—necessary to connect trauma
with effective learning in general.

Throughout the rest of this book, I invite you to join me in a deeper exploration of many of these areas. Some may prove emotionally difficult,
but I hope in the end they will challenge and ultimately enlighten you. I
know from clinical experience that some readers will find the topic of
traumatic learning uncomfortable, and in some cases perhaps even
painful. Ultimately, this book is not about reliving one's past traumas, but
addressing the realities of traumatic learning, in order to find an alternative, equally effective way of learning with fewer debilitating side effects.
And yes, there are and always will be skeptics. I try to continuously remind myself that it is in the fire of skepticism and the critical thinking
process that new theories are tempered and better ones will arise. Some
teachers will inevitably see the shift from teaching to learning and trans-

formational discovery as difficult, maybe appalling, possibly even threatening. I know—I've seen it happen as I share with colleagues the neurobiological theory, method, and tenets. Not everyone will make the leap or will even want to. But some will, and it is my sincere hope that for those who accept the challenge, their "teaching" and the learners they touch will be better for it.

THE GAME IS AFOOT

In this book, our explorations will take us through some controversial issues, like whether suppressed memories actually exist, what intelligence in the physical sense is, and how a neurobiological understanding of effective learning affects what we know as truth. These explorations will lead us to some surprising, sometimes counterintuitive discoveries, like "better teaching curricula actually inhibit learning." The point is that it is time to move beyond the ideations, business, and politics of teaching, and to embrace the rapidly expanding field of neurobiological learning. The end result, I believe, will prove to be a fascinating and ultimately satisfying personal voyage of discovery, which after all is at the very heart of neurobiological learning.

Over the years, I have found evidence for a growing suspicion that, within the field of education and linguistics, "something wicked has been this way coming" for over 2000 years. Given a newly emerging understanding of traumatic learning and an explosion in noninvasive medical imaging (to which I devote a whole chapter in "plain English" later in this book), we at last have the opportunity to break the shackles of trauma that have bound us so tightly. Taken together within a neurobiological context, these contemporary "miracles" have opened a new frontier of learning.

A new learning theory and methodology will require both linguistic and educational frameworks within which it can be interpreted, applied, and evaluated. Neurobiological theory and method should, for example, be equally applicable to classroom learning as to individual tutoring, one of the oldest learning formats known, and distance learning, the newest and most rapidly growing form of learning today. This neurobiological theory, its methodology, and its tenets need to be tested alongside the myriad existing teaching theses and theories, in every possible manner and situation, in order to ensure that what we now think we know about exceptional learning actually applies to learning in general. It is from within such a crucible that, I believe, a truly complete neurobiological theory and method will emerge and will ultimately triumph.

In terms of this book, my goals are considerably more modest: to explore with the reader the fundamental principles that underlie exceptional, effective, traumatic learning; to sketch out a neurobiological theory that "makes sense" of it all; to describe resulting hypothetical deductions, which with further research should help us to evaluate and refine the theory and method; and to develop a sufficient field framework within which the tenets—the basic principles—of effective, nontraumatic learning might be successfully applied in the widest range of learning situations.

In the next chapter, we will begin our exploration of the current clinical, empirical, experimental, and experiential information surrounding traumatic learning.

A final word about Albert, the young child upon whom experiments to induce fear were conducted. The researchers had planned a series of detachment exercises, as a way of removing Albert's conditioned emotional responses. "Unfortunately Albert was taken from the hospital the day the above tests were to be made. Hence the opportunity of building up an experimental technique by means of which we could remove the [traumatically] conditioned emotional responses was denied us."

Chapter Two

It All Begins with Traumatic Learning

Ever since the famous philosopher and teacher Plato broke from the Socratic tradition and formed his famed Academy 2000 years ago, the issue of "effective" teaching, learning, and education has been with us. The question is particularly relevant in our modern world, where the "business" of public as well as private education and the parents who generally pay for it demand academic as well as fiscal accountability. That effective teaching and learning is an issue is easy to determine: Just click on the "education" section of any Internet news site.

Education has experienced repeated cycles of intensive reexamination, the teaching of language, English, and English as a subsequent language notwithstanding. But why in over 2000 years hasn't this issue been solved and laid to rest? What is it that keeps eluding us? Perhaps we humans are all just so intimately immersed in individual lifelong learning and parenting that we have trouble seeing the forest for the trees. Or, perhaps trauma simply obscures trauma. Or, could it be that our ideas of learning, teaching, and education are actually at odds with what actually is and what we wish it to be?

Before becoming a professional linguist, I spent over twenty years as a practicing physician—first as a pediatrician and later as a public health/preventive medicine specialist. My personal as well as clinical subspecialty interest, however, was always in psychological recovery from trauma. I repeatedly observed the process of trauma survivors acquiring a whole new "language" just to communicate an experience outside the context of most of our own daily lives and to make some sense of it. I became increasingly interested in the processes involved in language acquisition and education. At the same time, it didn't take me long to notice a certain darkness that always seemed to lurk beneath trauma recovery. To my surprise, I soon discovered that same darkness lurking beneath language acquisition, learning, teaching, and education—the overwhelmingly powerful side effects of learning connected to control or intimidation—in nonmedical terms, violation, or violence; in medical terms, my old adversary, trauma.

My clinical work, in the end, proved to be a collection of intriguing detective stories. Like Sherlock Holmes, I was constantly in search of the underlying trauma that led to some problem, disease, condition, disability, or unwanted behavior for which I was consulted. They were interesting problems too, like recurring nightmares, obsessive-compulsive behaviors, sexual dysfunction, phobias, and anxiety attacks. In the course of these investigations, I became impressed that while only a few individuals sought help for these kinds of problems, their problems were in effect poignant expressions of a universal problem: How to deal with the immensity of "human suffering" that occurs when learning is accomplished through force imposed outside a learner's will. And what I was seeing was just the tip of the iceberg. This problem was both powerful and universal, touching not just the people I was seeing, who were aware of the problem, but virtually everyone—including me! In fact, the trees were everywhere, creating a dark forest surrounding us all.

When I retired from full time clinical practice and began my formal work in linguistics, I was surprised to see the familiar specter of traumatic learning reappear, over and over, in the guise of something educators often refer to as the "Holy Grail" of effective teaching. The problem in this context is that traumatic learning, this time in the form of impressing the ideas of one person, the teacher, onto another, the learner, was being so commonly employed that teachers were forever addressing the boundaries of effective teaching and learner abuse without realizing that they were, in fact, teaching traumatically. Whether it is about conveying more information more efficiently, or making the business of education more profitable, teaching as it is now practiced professionally throughout most of the world constantly utilizes the traumatic model we have so effectively assimilated from birth experience and have had reinforced throughout our lives!

Over time I became more aware of an underlying trauma, the trauma of traumas and one shared by all humans: the birth event. One of the classical signs of trauma, for example, is "erasure" of the original event—repression, if you will—of both a coherent understanding of the event and its attendant psychic pain. Perhaps nowhere is this more demonstrable than around the birth event. As a pediatrician, I repeatedly observed that birth trauma affected not only the newborn, who interestingly retains little memory of the birth event, but also the adult mother, who also retains little memory of the actual agony of childbirth. Odd. And I would like to point out that mothers are the primary source of language acquisition, behavioral imprinting, and early childhood cognitive learning for almost all humans—not just the learning of information, but the learning of how to learn—the penultimate teacher, by nature of her years of traumatic learning, a master in traumatic (effective) teaching and learning. When viewed in this manner, it is amazing that, given its ubiquitousness, we can reach a place where we are able to "see" traumatic learning even as it is occurring moment to moment in our lives.

A MOST INGENIOUS PARADOX

No one deliberately harms themselves. That's just common sense, and certainly conventional wisdom. Yet almost every day we read in the newspapers and see on television examples of people who seem to thrive on suffering, sadists who seem to enjoy hurting others, and even masochists who seem to invite others to hurt them. Then again, on careful reflection we have probably all known someone who seems caught up in this phenomenon: the friend who endlessly dates the wrong type, or the entrepreneur who repeatedly snatches financial defeat from the jaws of victory. And while we're at it, millions gladly and expectantly tune in to watch the next episode of their favorite television "soap"—all about endless cycles of suffering. Drug addiction, reckless driving, overeating, and suicide. Put in this way, those seemingly uncommon, exceptional examples of traumatic, violational learning I was investigating suddenly seemed not so uncommon—and frighteningly so!

But wait a moment: What makes trauma traumatic is supposed to be that it is an exception to the rule—unusual—so unusual, in fact, that it requires an entirely new language in order to "express the inexpressible." How can it be both unusual and yet so common? This doesn't make sense.

It's a paradox, and a most unusual paradox at that—one that affects all human lives—and because of our inability to see it, it can control our very lives, and thereby even collective human destiny.

Now that our eyes are a little more open, let's take a closer look at three examples of traumatic learning and try to see the role this process might be playing right now in our lives.

ETERNITY IN A GRAIN OF SAND

Consider for a moment "J.T.," a 38-year-old female office worker, seeking to rid herself of some unwanted obsessive and compulsive behaviors. During her process of recovery, she identified a specific traumatic event that occurred at about six years of age in rich, verifiable, though fragmentary detail. For her, these details—smells, images, sounds, tactile sensations, and feelings—clearly surrounded a powerful learning event that signaled the beginning of many of the unwanted behaviors.

Upon extensive investigation, some of the 32-year-old details of the traumatic learning event were found to have been nearly perfectly recalled. Total—what we call "eidetic"—recall of sensory fragments of a supposedly "forgotten" traumatic event is a hallmark of traumatic learning. Just the uncovering of the traumatic event proved to be the impetus needed to begin changing the unwanted behaviors. The numerous, eidetic, neurosensory memory fragments helped her to eventually identify the person, place, time, and nature of the traumatic learning event that had so profoundly affected her life.

Eidetic recall has been documented in women who were sexually abused as children, but it isn't limited by gender, age, circumstances, or weapon. Take for example "W.G.," a 30-year-old male, who suddenly began to slowly recover eidetic memories of what seemed to be multiple physical and psychological violations that had occurred 26 years earlier. W.G.'s memories started a "domino effect" of recall. When he asked other family members, including the suspected perpetrator, if they could verify what he was remembering, they were able to verify some of the memories, but more importantly, they soon began to recall more memory fragments from their own experience of the events. Somehow they had forgotten what they were now remembering, breaking their own rule that "if it's in the past, leave it in the past."

Initially, W.G. was quite anxious over the number and intensity of the eidetic memory fragments that were continuing to surface. In fact, the anxiety wasn't so much over whether what he was remembering was correct or true, but over its implication: the very fact that physical and psychological abuse by a significant family member had occurred.

At first he held strongly to an alternative explanation—that he had been abducted by aliens. Only later, when sufficient details were retrieved, was he able to confront and eventually verify, first from the family and later from the perpetrator, that it had really happened as he was remembering it. W.G.'s recovery challenged listeners, including myself, to separate eidetic memories (e.g., that the perpetrator seemed to act mechanically, without emotion) from its associations ("I felt like I no longer had control of my body; the perpetrator seemed inhuman") and interpretation ("I was being abducted by an alien"). Some listeners actually "took sides," as if their votes could somehow protect him from or alter the pain he was feeling, and as if *interpretation*, like eidetic recall, had to be "true," or even more disturbing, "false."

And how false was his interpretation, actually? His eidetic memories had helped three other members of his family, including the alleged perpetrator, recover their own repressed memories of their parts in the traumatic events, which in turn further validated his memory of the traumatic learning events. Much later, W.G. had his answer about whether the trauma had occurred, and even who played what roles in the events.

Unfortunately, I have found that traumatic learning events rarely occur singly, simply, or in isolation. For example, "S.W.," a 45-year-old male, entered recovery seeking to understand why feelings that were coming up for him while working professionally with abused children seemed resistant to the routine, end-of-the-day psychological debriefing. In fact, eidetic memories of psychological, physical, and sexualized assault and battery that had occurred more than twenty distinct times, from two to eighteen years of age, began surfacing in vivid dreams.

Was this a case of extreme empathy (countertransference, medically speaking), or was it "real"? What made it all seem so "unreal" was surfacing memories of multiple kinds and times of trauma.

Actually, this was not the first or last time I encountered this situation—
that is, more than one episode of more than one kind of traumatic violation. While the majority of cases I experienced were with adults struggling
with remembering and resolving childhood traumas, S.W.'s case also illustrates that traumatic learning is not limited to early childhood trauma.
Finally, while some clearly significant data and information were never
really repressed ("Everyone, even my next-door neighbors, knew my father was physically and sexually abusive to me and other family members
on at least one particular occasion—well, actually many others as well"),
the overwhelming number and variety of associations from multiple
episodes eventually led to multiple interpretations of the abuse, including
imagining it all, self-abuse, latent homosexual tendencies, abuse by other
family members, and even abuse by nonfamily members such as aliens,
Satanists, secret societies, and the military, all of which eventually resur-
faced 25 years after the abuses stopped, and interestingly at the time of the
death of the actual perpetrator.

MODUS OPERANDI

Regardless of the trauma, it was demonstrated over and over again that
people learn effectively, almost passionately, from traumatic experiences.
Having acknowledged this, I was now in the unique position of being able
to further consider various other attributes of this bitter form of learning
and their lasting effects. I could see the power of traumatic learning, but I
was especially interested in *why* people would compulsively repeat a
painful experience again and again.

As demonstrated above, denial (or more accurately, repression) is a
common means of coping with abuse for everyone involved: offenders,
victims, even nonoffending observers, partners, and professional witnesses like therapists, who smell, hear, see, feel, taste, or experience in
their own gut or muscles some aspect of the trauma in its retelling. The
trauma doesn't end. Even in the retelling or recovery, it continues to exact its toll.

Repressing any part of so powerful a process is not easy to do. It takes
considerable energy to keep track of things that one doesn't want to re-

member while letting everything else come in or out of memory "naturally," to keep constantly alert for any associations that might accidentally allow any one of millions of repressed traumatic memory fragments to suddenly escape into consciousness, and to keep quickly plugging every new crack in the memory dam through which a painful memory fragment might suddenly escape. The medical term for this effort is called depression, and the energy involved is almost unimaginable. Is it any wonder that depressed individuals are usually chronically exhausted and tired? Whether the memory fragments are "successfully" repressed at the expense of one's own energy or with the assistance of medication, as time goes on, the cracks increase and many are unable to hold back the dreaded flood of memories.

But there is another aspect of traumatic memory that is even more debilitating: Trauma survivors rarely maintain a complete memory of the trauma. This is part of the apparent paradox of eidetic recall. An incest survivor, for example, may experience many odd or disturbing memory fragments, with little or no cohesive memory of the incident itself. As memories are recovered that point to a cohesive event, the pain associated with the details makes it clear why they were repressed. This is, however, learning at its most powerful. The pain of the learning experience literally dominates the way a person will or will not think about it. It's also one of the cruelest attributes of traumatic learning, confusing the learner with sleight of hand: "now you see it, now you don't."

This *apparent* paradox of traumatic learning is actually the key to understanding effective learning: Most, but not all, trauma survivors have eidetic memories surrounding the event. At the same time, most have few cohesive memories, at least as we commonly think of them. It was while attempting to resolve this apparent paradox, these "exceptions to the general rule" of how memory should or should not work, that my own insights into exceptional learning began to emerge.

UNIMPEACHABLE CLUES

Whether from experience or formal education, a common question is "Why can't you learn this?" In many instances, however, a far better question would be "What are you trying to unlearn?" Traumatic learning experiences evoke eidetic recall . . . near-perfect, moment-to-moment, fragmentary, neurosensory recall. Many traumatically induced eidetic memories, however, because of the pain associated with their recall, are repressed. They do live on—in fact, my experience is that they never really "go away"—just beneath the surface of consciousness.

The right stimulus, what we clinicians call a trigger, is all that is necessary for a crack to open and sometimes for the dam to break. The explosion of a space shuttle or the death of Elvis Presley, for example, can lead us back to recall in perfect detail some neurosensory details of where we were when we first heard about it (e.g., the feel of warm sunlight on our skin from the sun at the beach where we heard the announcement), what we were doing, or how we were feeling.

Through my work with traumatic learning, I have begun to probe these experiences, and have begun to see that traumatic learning is more common than most of us would suspect. It is, in fact, a subconscious part of a variety of common experiences—ones we don't usually think of as exceptional or unusual, though they clearly meet all the criteria for a traumatic learning event. Consider, for example, the millions of episodes of cultural violence that permeate the news, sports, and even aggressive business practices like "hostile takeovers." In fact, with eyes wide open, traumatic learning opportunities seem to be everywhere.

Most people today grudgingly acknowledge that the price of peace and prosperity is traumatic learning. Consider, for example, the effort that our military exerts in "training" soldiers to kill—to inflict trauma. What and how do virtually all American males over eighteen years of age learn during this period of training? And if deployed, what do they learn? It is not a surprise to me that random shootings occur in a civilized society like ours, but rather that they occur so infrequently, given what they have traumatically learned! It would be easy to blame it all on the military, but consider for another moment some other aspects of our lives: Consider business training. The point of business is to accumulate wealth—money. "Business is war." Executive training is directed toward control and intimidation, and the means commonly employed include advertising (deceit), marketing (control and intimidation), and even offers that one "cannot refuse" (fear and intimidation). But now let's expand this to education.

The bottom line is that teaching is all about how efficiently and effectively a "teacher" can clone his or her "ideas" in the minds of "students." A good portion of teacher training is focused on how to control students' attention; teachers use grades to control student activities through fear and intimidation, and effective classroom management is always a hot topic of discussion. More interestingly, teachers are taught to teach in the same manner. I well recall many university colleagues I have worked with over the years telling me the fear that their own comprehensive examinations generated; how, in many cases, they were driven to tears during their dissertation defense. My own experience during internship and residency was traumatic—even today I can recall various fragments of the experience when a particular sensory trigger, like the smell of hospital disinfectant, presents itself.

One thing that especially caught my attention was that those who witnessed violence often experienced more difficulty with recovery than those who were the actual targets and receivers of the violence. For example, "T.S.," a 42-year-old male who, as a child, had repeatedly witnessed but was powerless to stop the repeated sexual assault and battery of a sibling by an adult authority figure, took much longer to redirect his anger from himself to the perpetrator than did the victim.

I have long suspected that socially sanctioned, public witnessing of violence, for example, at theaters, may be more damaging to viewers and more likely to be compulsively reenacted than direct trauma. Even our most "nontraumatic" social events, for example, Christmas for some, have their own form of torture for those who don't feel happy but believe that they should be as happy as everyone else seems during this holiday. In short, in an increasingly complicated and socially challenging society, exposure to witnessed, potential, and random violence is not only commonplace, but may in fact be more damaging than we would like to believe.

THE GREATEST TRAUMA NEVER TOLD

I wish that this were all I had to say about the perversity and pervasiveness of traumatic learning. Unfortunately, it is not. My clinical investigations into traumatic learning, which began when I was a pediatric resident, soon began to draw me further back in time, from the often elusive primary traumatic learning event to what I have now come to consider the basic, common human element of traumatic learning: the birth event.

One of the classical signs of trauma is "erasure" of the event as a whole—repression of both the totality of the event *as it really was*, and its psychic pain. Perhaps nowhere is this more demonstrable than with birth. I was originally taught in residency that newborns feel little pain, or at least a different, diminished form of pain than adults—a fashionable idea that was not supported by clinical observation from the very first time I had to draw blood to the cries of a newborn. I was also taught that their nervous system was not sufficiently developed to learn and remember the trauma. Yet I repeatedly observed that birth trauma affected not only the newborn, but also and equally the adult mother, both of whom quickly fragment and forget the experience of childbirth as it really was, to the point that the mother soon becomes ready to "obsessively" or at least "compulsively" repeat the trauma.

As a human, I realize how important this traumatic learning mechanism is—without it, or better, with total eidetic recall of the entire event, we might cease elective procreation. Birthrates would decline, except during exceptional times. As a species, we would begin searching out nonprocreative forms of physical gratification and intimacy with oneself, the same gender, across societal barriers, or even across species. We might begin "devolving," in effect, electively ceasing to exist as a species. This may sound like a "Mad Max" nightmare, but I challenge you to think about the current state of humanity.

But there's more. We've each experienced this primal traumatic learning event naked, alone, and without reason. The best that could be said is that we experienced separation from a protective environment, familiar sounds (like the ever-present heartbeat of God), and at least some kind of sense of stability during the nine-month eternity inside the womb. Is this where our wellspring of hope and an almost universal, tightly held vision of God, "heaven," and "hell" come from during our one, physical lifetime?

It is impossible to completely erase experience. Determining why *we think* something happened is often the closest we get to making sense of trauma, and a newborn's knowledge and wisdom about the world into which it has just been thrust are exceptionally limited. I believe there is a good reason why therapy surrounding the birth event is sometimes called primal scream therapy.

And need I point out that the mother, who is a co-participant in this traumatic event, will be the principal source of primary imprinted and early childhood learning for almost all humans—not just learning; but learning how to learn; that is, in many respects, learning to become a master of effective, traumatic, violational learning *from an experience that must have triggered many of her own repressed memories of birth*. When considered in this way, is it any wonder we might be so blindsided to traumatic learning and its effects? It is amazing that we have any ability at all to step outside these primal traumatic life experiences, and even more amazing to me that one can "see" traumatic learning *in a book* like this one for what it is! There's no doubt, whether "alien" or human, about the meteoric impact of traumatic learning, especially when it's so clearly overwhelming as to be unspeakable.

RITUAL

When something happens to us, it is our nature to try to make sense of it. This is not a kind of innate program. I believe it results from the "Biggest Bang" of our entire lives: birth trauma, which was experienced naked, alone, and without any idea of why it was happening, only that it was entirely outside our control.

Spectacular claims have recently surfaced in the press and courts regarding false memories often concerned with ritualized trauma—ritual abuse. The very term invokes fear, darkness, death, and evil. The sensational part usually surrounds whether a bizarre crime was committed as it has been interpreted—cohesively reassembled—by the state from victim(s') or witness(es') eidetically recalled fragments. The sensation *is* the show—the reality of ritualized trauma is almost always what is eventually placed on trial.

Actually, ritualized trauma is any traumatic learning event that includes a prescribed ceremony over which the victim feels he or she has little control. In ritualized trauma the learner reaches a point where saying no is not only ineffectual, it has no meaning and could lead to increased danger. In a more general sense, ritualized traumatic learning includes formally repeated acts that eventually result in violations by oneself against oneself. This is, I believe, the true basis of its sensationalism—that and the fact

that, given the above definition, ritualized trauma is everything but uncommon, and by its very nature one of the most personally painful crimes
imaginable. It is so powerful, painful, unforgettable, unforgivable, and un-
believable because it is a crime against oneself.

Ritualized trauma is generally held to be very unusual—its unusualness
is considered by some to be a primary defining characteristic. But in fact
entire industries are built on the idea of ritualized, or if you prefer social-
ized, trauma. The blockbuster Hollywood film about Hannibal Lecter, a
fastidiously brilliant cannibal, seems to perfectly capture the mix of mind
and mayhem that most associate with ritualized abuse. Millions witnessed
this and other socially approved (rated) movies demonstrating ritualized
trauma in explicit detail. And consider for a moment other forms of socially allowed (carefully marketed, distributed, and in many cases publicly sold) ritualized trauma: smoking, alcoholism, prostitution, war, cir-
cumcision, corporal punishment, even professional sports, hunting, and
fishing.

Ritual introduces "outside" associations and interpretations, and ritualized trauma introduces them highly effectively, in association with other
traumatic or even nontraumatic learning objects. This is the very essence
of ritual. In effect, the witness, victim, or learner is left not only with his
or her fragmented, eidetic memories, associations, and interpretation(s) of
what happened, but also with an organized, meaningful interpretation provided from "outside" the fragmented experience, as well as additional associations and memories that internally validate it. Ritual adds yet another
dimension, and a very powerful one, especially when it occurs during or
immediately surrounding a traumatic learning event.

These observations, taken collectively, strongly suggest that traumatic
learning occurs in at least two and possibly more steps, levels, phases, or
dimensions: The first involves experiencing and recording the neurosensory data surrounding a traumatic act or events; this step or level involves
fragmentary but eidetic recall of neurosensory phenomena, data if you
will, involving the five classical senses (smells, sights, sounds, tastes, and
tactile sensations) as well as visceral or "gut" feelings based on neuromuscular sensations. Most of these are generated inside the body of the
learner in response to the traumatic experience.

The second involves the formation of various associations of these data
with any other data, associations, and interpretations available at the time,

to form "information" if you will. Associations include those made up by the learner and those introduced by perpetrators, interlocutors, and teachers. They also include the learner's "take" on what the others said, did, or experienced. An example of this would be the so-called Stockholm Syndrome, in which victims (or students) identify with a perpetrator, interlocutor, or teacher. Many people who were not direct targets of the events of 9/11/01 nonetheless shared in the trauma through association.

The third involves making some kind of meaningful sense of the myriad pieces of information—forging it all into one or more interpretations so that it doesn't seem so crazy and out of control (which it most likely seemed during the learning experience). Interpretations include those created by *or introduced into* the mind of the learner at or surrounding the time of the traumatic learning event, and those interjected later by the learner and others as they witness recall of the fragments and interpretations.

Traumatic learning, which at first seems a cataclysmic chaos, appears under clinical scrutiny to be a process that involves at least three and possibly more distinct learning steps, phases, or levels. There is a discernible method to the ever-present madness, if one can just leap outside it for even a brief moment and view it in its insidious totality. But are we in fact viewing its totality? While my mind kept saying, "Please! Yes! Surely this is enough!" the very muscles and sinews of my own body echoed, "No! There is still more. The voyage has only begun."

Chapter Three

Make Up Your Mind

PINK HERRINGS

Traumatically learned eidetic memories are often described as "vague and dreamlike" and come back in "bits and pieces." They are often like flashes in time (flashbacks), during which one accurately reexperiences the neurosensory pieces of the trauma. They can occur singly or massed together as visual, auditory, olfactory, tactile, gustatory, and feeling-based memories. Remembered together with associated feelings, they often seem overpowering or intellectually grandiose. In their own way, they are incredibly powerful. They can, for instance, be a portal of resurrection—a new life—either more deeply embedded in traumatic learning processes, or the impetus for breaking out of them.

When correctly viewed as what they are, trauma survivors often express fear not so much that they will come back, but that they will be lost before they can be reassociated and reinterpreted in a more meaningful context. My experience is that eidetic memories are rarely ever lost, and instead can be solicited repeatedly by discovering the initially unrecognized neurosensory or emotive trigger. In fact, the tendency to be recalled by the same or similar triggers can be quite vexing for many.

Consider these symptoms, expressed so poignantly by one survivor-learner dealing with a traumatic learning event from adulthood: "Ridiculous problems . . . walking down the block I'm in a perpetual cringe. I'm constantly stopping to let whoever is behind me pass: my body keeps expecting a blow from every side" (Weschler 1998, p. 162). My job for many years was tracing mystifying reactions like this one back to a repressed traumatic learning event. In the process, I discovered that in searching down and exposing these events, I was redefining the very idea of "learning."

First I had to try to figure out why some memories became fixed and forgotten, and how our mind struggles to hide these traumatic events in the most creative way possible. Like Alice, I was about to go down the Rabbit Hole. I supposed that there was no real choice: My patients had gone there ahead of me. Entering it was like joining a play created by another, in which I was not privy to the script, and which had been going on for innumerable years. Even after all my years of experience, it is still difficult to explain what it actually feels like. I try to be utterly transparent, to retain and focus my own tempered curiosity and keep my senses wide open, but not to give away the car keys, so to speak.

When encountered, traumatically induced memories are something akin to a ring around the tub: They don't seem to belong, but are tenaciously persistent. At first they seem to be red herrings—false or confusing clues thrown in to divert one's attention from the traumatic event. Of course in the end, when one associates and interprets them "correctly," they're not. Given these characteristics, I surmised that some portion of traumatic learning—the learned data or object—is subject to eidetic recall, while another portion—the learner's interpretation or meaning of the learning event, which always seems so vividly real—is not eidetic, and in fact can be quite malleable.

THE ARMAGEDDON FACTOR

According to the definitions above, even in our modern, psychologically savvy society, ritualized traumatic learning, one of the most powerful forms of traumatic learning identified thus far, is quite common to teachers and educational institutions alike.

It can be difficult to "see" and even more difficult to acknowledge socially, even when proved beyond a shadow of a doubt, but it remains a cornerstone of effective learning, mirrored and reinforced, even in children, by the literally millions of moment-to-moment traumatic experiences that surround us and impact our lives. Yet its full impact was not evident to me until I began to run across accounts of a traumatic event, not unlike 9/11 in final impact, that affected most of Brazil back in 1979—an event that shed yet more light on the nature of ritualized traumatic learning. Initially published under the title *Brasil: Nunca Mais* (English translation: "Brazil: Never Again"), an extraordinary book about a nationwide rash of ritualized traumatic events that occurred during the political tenure of a Brazilian military junta suddenly appeared in bookstores all over Brazil on July 15, 1985. It subsequently appeared in English under the title *Torture in Brazil* and was expanded on in *A Miracle, A Universe* in 1990.

Most of our knowledge of ritualized traumatic learning comes from information uncovered and reinterpreted long after the original traumatic event. Until these books, there never existed a complete written record of ritualized traumatic learning as it was occurring, in the words of both the perpetrator and victim, that undeniably preserved their perspectives at the time of the event. *Brasil: Nunca Mais* summarized data from *all* of the complete, official, verbatim transcripts of *both* victims and perpetrators of torture at each victim's final military trial, just prior to a "final solution"—a continuation of the original traumatic events in which freshly remembered data, associations, and interpretations were recorded, checked, and acknowledged by signature of the perpetrator and/or the court. This book presented the first window into the traumatic learning process *as it was occurring* . . . and, in this case, shed light on the question "Does what a victim-learner learns in ritualized, traumatic learning match torturer-teacher records?" The answer was an emphatic "Yes!" with regard to neurosensory details, and a "Sometimes, but not necessarily so" with regard to associations and interpretation.

The effects of the publication of these books, their contributions to recovery and resulting insights into ritualized traumatic learning, in my opinion cannot be overemphasized. Here, for the first time, was incontrovertible proof of how ritualized traumatic learning actually occurred in context—caught and legally recorded "in the act." From a contemporary point of view, these publications vividly affirm the veracity of learners' eidetic memory fragments and the power of the perpetrator, teacher, or interlocutor role, both early and late, in interpreting the data. There are other windows into trauma. For example, after the Columbine school shootings, the public widely interpreted school violence as "epidemic," when in fact it was exactly the opposite: School crime had been steadily decreasing. But never has anything been of the scale, impact, and detail of *Brasil: Nunca Mais*.

The book and its sequels contributed another, equally important insight into the nature of ritualized traumatic learning: It identified confession, an important, combined sensory, motor, and intellectual response that occurs when a learner fully accepts another's interpretation of the traumatic learning event, whether or not it matches the learner's interpretation, as a halfway point in disintegration.

It's not difficult to understand why a learner might be willing to discard his or her own interpretation—medically speaking, to dissociate—and yet accept or even substitute another's interpretation. The upshot of this in contemporary education is the cloning and insertion of a teacher's beliefs into the learners' minds. Most would agree that when these beliefs are successfully reintegrated, effective learning has occurred. Yet from a slightly different point of view, this could and has been viewed as intellectual rape.

From just a little more radical point of view, one could say that learning comes at the expense of a partial dissolution of the learner's self. In the extreme, it constitutes the spiritual opposite of living, that is, death itself. Whether or not you accept these increasingly dramatic points of view, there should be little doubt that, presented in this context, traumatic learning, especially ritualized traumatic learning, constitutes a form of violation that should be beyond our darkest imagination.

What is most important here is that this kind of learning *isn't* beyond our darkest imagination; it is occurring daily throughout our lives. In common terms, ritualized traumatic learning is not only powerful, effective, and common, it also has the capability of destroying a learner's most precious personal, social, political, and spiritual treasures—the inner child, identity, ego, self, and soul.

In fact, traumatic learning carries with it, at the least, a quadruple liability. It is capable of invoking individually destructive learning in four and possibly more collateral learning systems: the *sympathetic nervous system* (the electrically mediated, locally targeted portion of the "fight or flight" reflex system); the *neuroendocrine system* (the hormonally mediated, whole body–targeting portion of the "fight or flight" reflex system); the *cerebellar system* that focuses on the learning of rhythms and patterns; and the *thalamic system* (the neural gateway deep inside the brain where the brain selects what will, in fact, be learned).

THE SINS OF THE FATHERS

Life or death survival requires quick, unconscious, primitive, whole-body reactions that are generally nonvolitional. Thinking about various ways to defend yourself when a tiger is attacking simply takes too long! The "thinkers" die; the "doers" may survive, depending on what they actually do. If they do something and they survive, survival learning says that what they did made them survive, and that they should do it again in a similar situation. Fast reactions in response to a particular neurosensory object are called reflexes. Reflexes can be simple, like jerking your hand from a hot oven, or can involve multiple, complex, often highly integrated sensory-mental-motor patterns, like your reactions when someone shouts "Watch out!" Most involve the mind and body (some say body-mind-spirit), and the "best" ones—the ones that work to greatest advantage—are often common to both humans and animals.

Some primitive survival reflexes appear "hardwired" before birth, without apparent traumatic antecedent. Consider for example the head-turning reflex, yawning reflex, rooting reflex, infantile-separation-cry reflex, righting reflex, swimming reflex, and freedom reflex. Most animals, including humans, apparently develop a unique set of primitive, learned, sensorimotor, stimulus-response, survival-oriented behaviors of their own. These reflexes are believed to originate from traumatic learning events experienced during birth, the immediate postnatal period, and probably gestation. The catchword is "apparently"; the truth is that the whole story has yet to be fully understood.

All reflexes, according to the famous Russian scientist Ivan Pavlov, are part of a "first system" of common communication (language being the second). In this sense, survival reflexes look a lot like traumatically learned behaviors. In fact, survival reflexes are usually invoked in the very first moments of a possible "fight or flight" situation. Soon consciousness becomes tightly focused (the biomedical term is "constricted") on incoming neurosensory data and information, any of which might quickly and unconsciously initiate a previously learned survival reflex that might provide a survival advantage. "Normal" body functions like eating and digestion slow down or stop altogether. The heart beats faster. Breathing becomes more efficient. The senses suddenly seem sharper, clearer, and more sensitive. Your field of vision widens, even as things not being focused on become hazy. Time seems to slow as excitement builds. Muscles get ready to do things we normally think they are incapable of. Pain diminishes. We get edgy, as if every action were controlled by the finest of hair triggers. This particular combination of effects prepares an organism for maximal, quick, fight-or-flight response, and incidentally provides an enhanced platform for learning and acquiring new survival reflexes. The neurobiological system that is being invoked here is sympathetic to our "fight or flight" survival needs. Without it we can't live long enough to learn what we wish to learn. We simply learn what we have to learn, quickly and efficiently; if we don't, we die. Those who live, have a new set of reflexes hardwired into them.

Sympathetic learning is intense. It requires considerable energy and is time limited. The body sacrifices a lot in order to divert sufficient energy to sympathetic learning, as for example the ability to marshal a coordinated immune response. But it can do this for only a short time before it takes a toll on the body as a whole. During sympathetic system learning, the body, so to speak, will pay any price for gasoline. But it can't do it for very long.

While sympathetic activation seems to occur in a matter of minutes, what actually occurs is that the neuroelectrical components, the sympathetic nervous system per se, is activated first. This activates the hormonal components, or adrenal cortical axis, which floods the body with "fight or flight" hormones. These in turn rev up the volume and speed of the whole nervous system, including the neuroelectrical components. This then further activates the hormonal components, and so forth. The entire traumatic learning system is now on highest alert.

Earlier we explored the traumatic learning world of Albert B., clearly a victim-learner, for whom each of these systems must have quickly amplified the effectiveness of the traumatic learning event. *Albert B. eventually learned much, much more than what was initially taught.* But was Albert the only one affected? Was he really the only learner? Our knowledge of the sympathetic system strongly suggests that traumatic learning occurs in both prey *and* predator, victim *and* perpetrator, learner *and* teacher.

Now hold that thought for a moment, and let's turn back in time to two classic teacher-learner experiments in effective teaching that involve learner-teacher learning: The first is psychologist Philip Zimbardo's infamous "Stanford Prison Experiment"; the second, social psychologist Stanley Milgram's experiments with authority.

The following is excerpted from a 1997 Stanford University News Service article by Kathleen O'Toole. About two dozen young, healthy, psychologically normal, male college students were selected from a group responding to an advertisement in the *Palo Alto Times* to participate in the experiment. Each was randomly assigned to be either a guard or a prisoner.

"Prisoners" were "arrested" in their homes on August 17, 1971, by Palo Alto police, booked at a real jail, then blindfolded and driven to a makeshift prison in the basement of a Stanford University building. "Guards" were given uniforms and instructed that they were to maintain control without the use of violence. On only the second day, the guards tightened control when they suddenly perceived their authority being challenged, and over the next few days they became increasingly violent in their control of their charges. The nature and details of the violations, while sensational, are not important. The experiment was prematurely terminated after less than a week, after complaints from a colleague who witnessed the turn of events firsthand made Zimbardo suddenly realize what was happening to the people in the study as well as himself.

Zimbardo, as well as various participants and observers, later wrote extensively about the experience, including the difficult issue of how ordinary, "good" people were so quickly transformed into perpetrators. But what struck me as I read about the details of the experiment was that while the experiment was ostensibly about prisons, guards, and prisoners, it was also a lightly veiled model of the processes involved in classical teaching. While Zimbardo's experiment clearly answered the question about how easily violation could enter into a teaching situation, an even more frightening question was, once invoked, exactly how far would the violations go?

Prior to this, around 1965, Yale University social psychologist Stanley Milgram had performed a series of experiments, reported in detail in his now-classic book *Obedience to Authority*, in which some ordinary residents of New Haven were told to deliver increasingly powerful electric shocks to a stranger while observing the victim—a stranger they were informed had no reason to deserve it. The victim was actually an actor who did not receive any shocks, but this was not revealed to the subjects until after the experiment.

Milgram reported that a shocking two-thirds of the test subjects were willing to inflict up to 450 volts, labeled "danger—severe shock," while watching the victim protesting pitifully. Like some of Zimbardo's guard-subjects, many of Milgram's test subjects were reportedly anguished when the experiment was revealed in its entirety and they had to come to grips with the unrealized extent of the darkness within themselves. But *this realization came afterwards—it hadn't stopped them from doing it and, once engaged, rapidly escalating the violence.*

After studying these experiments, it was not difficult to realize why teachers must work so diligently to avoid abuse in the classroom. At the same time I realized how, given the nature of teaching, it would be difficult if not impossible to actually accomplish this. And we know now that what learner and teacher effectively learn can be quite difficult to unlearn. Both the potential for and the extent of damage that can result from teaching and traumatic learning left little doubt in my mind that, while clearly effective, they needed to be not just overhauled, but entirely replaced.

But how? And with what? Unfortunately, neither study delved deeper into the biochemical, hormonal, or neuroanatomical systems that were being engaged. It was, therefore, still not clear exactly how teaching and traumatic learning worked their destructive curses. Without this knowledge, it was possible that whatever was proposed to replace it might actually cause more unwitting harm. It was time to return, once again, to the actual processes of traumatic learning. It's time to pick up where we left off: with the sympathetic learning system.

Some say that the sympathetic learning system is the very heart of Darwinian survival-of-the-fittest doctrine—a hot-as-the-sun, pyrotechnic melting pot where effective, new, learned behaviors result. Actually, as we shall soon see, it's often actually more like a sudden Ice Age, in which simultaneously occurring neuromuscular reactions and neurosensory fragments (that may or may not have any rational or causal relationship at all) are frozen together in an eternal, cryogenic library.

I have, in fact, observed both of these survival modes: the classical "fight or flight" state, described in detail above, and a state of frozen immobilization that seems to occur when the trauma and/or traumatic learning event do not sufficiently activate any survival reflex(es) at all. Perhaps the sensations are entirely new to the victim, as for example sexual activity might be to a five-year-old. On the other hand, perhaps the traumatic event does not quickly resolve, or the breadth or intensity of the neu-rosensory input is simply overwhelming. In fact, some survivors, like S.W., reported neither fighting nor fleeing. Instead, S.W. reported a "freezing" of all his major motor systems, not unlike shock. And why not? Trauma is, after all, a major shock to the mind, body, and spirit.

This second survival mode appears to initiate an even more enhanced, more persistent form of traumatic learning. In this mode, the victim's thoughts become separated—mentally dissociated—from his or her sen-sations, and usually from the learning act as well. Although unable to mount a motor response, neurosensory data still appear to be eidetically recorded. These data, however, are internally linked—associated—with any neurosensory data, even disconnected thoughts, emotions, or feelings that were being recorded at the same time. For example, a feeling of panic during rape might be associated with the chirping of a bird (that just hap-pened to have been heard at the same time). The chirping of the bird is now frozen together with a feeling of panic. But because of the nature of traumatic learning, the memory of the rape *as well as* the chirping is re-pressed. Later, when any similar chirp is heard, it is again instantly re-pressed, and a feeling of panic surfaces: What the survivor experiences is that sometimes, out of the blue, he or she experiences panic attacks. Through detective work, the link to bird chirps might be uncovered. What seems like craziness is, in effect, not at all crazy *if you know the whole story*. Actually it's just sympathetically enhanced, traumatic learning!

Effective learning, as I have observed it, is composed of at least three components, phases, or steps: The first is the now-familiar record of ei-detic neurosensory data fragments; the second is reinforcement of the data through association with felt, linked, but often disparate thoughts, emo-tions, and feelings; and the third is the assignment of "meaning" or inter-pretation to the whole "crazy" experience. It is at the neurosensory data and associative levels that effective learning is introduced and firmly an-chored in memory. These "memories," however, are quite different from usual memories. Survivors often refer to traumatic memories less like cognate ideas and more as "muscle" or "body" memories—more like mixed-up, sensory-based, highly charged "gut" reflexes—in medical terms, kines-thetic memories.

It is worth mentioning here the *brain-stem learning system*. Sometimes erroneously called the "reptilian brain," it has been credited with control of primitive sexual, territorial, and survival instincts and regulation of automatic behaviors. In fact, as mentioned above, invocation of the neuro-electrical and hormonally mediated sympathetic learning systems is more than sufficient to account for most acquired, primitive reflexive behaviors (other than, for example, breathing). Although the idea of having a dinosaur inside each of us is seductively empowering, we are not reptiles, and like dragons, fairies, and goblins under the bed at night, they are but intriguing ideas—phantoms—with no physical substance.

MUSIC OF THE SPHERES

Traumatic learning, on the other hand, appears to occur with regard to another kind of learning object-data: rhythm—repetitive patterns of sounds, sights, smells, tastes, tactile sensations, and "gut" sensations or feelings—sometimes separate, but more commonly all mixed together. In this case, it is not so much the raw neurosensory object-data as it is any underlying repetitive pattern that is subject to learning, traumatic or otherwise.

I found that with work, trauma survivors are often able to identify neurosensory object-data patterns that "trigger" traumatically learned sensory or kinesthetic "memories" and behavioral reflexes. S.W., for example, despite being an incest survivor with many unwanted traumatic memories and reflexes, was a model citizen: He largely abstained from the otherwise widespread and socially acceptable practices of drinking alcoholic beverages and smoking, and even generally declined the eating of animal flesh. What particularly interested me was *why* he chose these wonderful behaviors. He was not a member of any group, church, or religion that espoused these beliefs. He did, in fact, try smoking a pipe (but never cigarettes) for a while, and drinking wine (though he complained of "going to sleep" instead of being more affable after a glass or two), and he enjoyed an occasional very, very well-done steak. In fact, he strongly disliked being around people who engaged in all three—the drinking of beer or whiskey, accompanied by cigarette smoking and the eating of rare, "bloody" meats—even more so *in that order*, which he found so disgusting that it often "made his palms sweat." But it seemed to me a bit odd—there seemed an unnaturally stilted, traumatic sense about it all.

During recovery, S.W. began to "remember" some interesting characteristics that the various traumatic events often had in common: First, the perpetrator was a heavy drinker, who commonly consumed a bottle of whiskey and several six-packs of beer at the beginning of a drinking bout. When traumatically engaged, he almost always smelled like sour beer and whiskey. In fact, his "habit" was to drink heavily just prior to engaging S.W. in a traumatic event. Second, the perpetrator was a heavy smoker: two to five packs a day. When traumatically engaged, he almost always "reeked of smoke." In fact, the perpetrator's "habit" was to begin to chain-smoke as the effects of the alcohol took hold. Some of the most traumatic events occurred after several days of binge drinking, chain smoking, and family disruption by the perpetrator.

During these bouts, it was his "habit" to add a raw egg to his beer, or to eat hamburger tartar—raw and bloody—openly in front of the family, including the victim. Each of the conditions separately created traumatic memories linked to the ensuing abuse. But together, in this particular order, the effect was considerably heightened.

It was, in fact, through this rather complex example that I discovered that rhythm—the perceived order of neurosensory elements in time and space—was actually another traumatic learning *object*. At the heart of rhythm is time, or at the very least, time-flow perception. The *cerebellar brain system*, which focuses on rhythms and patterns, is different from the cerebral and sympathetic brain systems in terms of the kinds of neurosensory data and information that are stored, but similar in terms of the process and qualities of what is learned traumatically. Music and dance, which are both grounded in rhythm, are considered categorical areas of learning that are at least partially under cerebellar brain system control. In fact, any form of learning, including traumatic learning, that has a rhythmic component, for example ritual, would be as well. While the whole concept of rhythmic enhancement of traumatic learning may seem novel, it isn't. Ancient Greek Pyrrhic music and dances, for example, were used for war training and preparation and have been used both tactically and strategically in warfare.

For me, it isn't so much a wonder how unique each of us is. It's more amazing to me that we are able to tolerate each other long enough to procreate and sometimes even communicate as well. Similar incredulity led

Dr. Walter Freeman, a professor of cellular and molecular biology at the University of California, Berkeley, to question how animals and humans can share the world outside themselves when all they know is what they have reconstructed for themselves within their own brains. It is here that symbolistic, particularly rhythmic, "music" probably comes into play.

Perhaps it is not so much the data that we share, as a common, rhythmic musicality that underlies our individual perceptions of similar traumatic events. Recall, if you will, an earlier morning when, tired, you mumbled something to your partner or mate like "mninghroo" and he or she replied back, "I'm great, how about you?" What was the listener really responding to? Clear, specific words (grammar)? Their obvious order (structure)? Interspersed linkers, delimiters, and other kinds of discourse markers? Or a rhythm and musical pattern? Like the character Mumbles in the Batman stories, it's surprising what we are actually able to hear and understand *in spite of* grammar and structure! And what new father or mother tells a newborn baby who is smiling and cooing softly, "No! Subject first, verb next! And use the correct verb tense if you want my attention now!" From the very beginning, we communicate primarily using melodious rhythms.

Up to now, our attention has been focused almost exclusively on data processing and storage. My clinical experience with trauma survivors, however, strongly supports the existence of at least one additional learning system: a functional area that affects all of the above systems by selecting what will or won't be learned. For example, more memories can often be elicited from trauma survivors using specialized techniques such as hypnosis or eye movement desensitization and reprocessing (EMDR).

It is something like shaking a tree and seeing what else falls out of it after first picking the obvious fruit. At the same time, applying these techniques is sometimes followed by a period of reduced number and strength of flashbacks. As a result, traumatic reenactments diminish, *without the rerepression of the triggering memories*. It is as if one were suddenly accessing and changing not the areas where data and associations are stored, but the learning gateway itself. There is growing evidence that this gateway may be located in the midbrain area of the brain—in medical jargon, the combined *thalamic, hypothalamic, and/or hippocampal brain system(s)*.

Furthermore, recent advances in clinical psychopharmacology suggest that certain chemicals such as naturally occurring dopamine, serotonin, and endorphins directly affect the quantity, quality, and nature of traumatic memories. Similarly, drugs such as marijuana, cocaine, and amphetamines can play a role in traumatic learning.

Environmental factors such as how threatening a learning event is perceived to be (for example, whether it is perceived as just irritating or outright terrifying); the victim's physical condition as well as character (e.g., easily excitable); his or her available energy, equilibrium, and physical-mental-spiritual reserves; available supportive resources; the victim's collective life experiences and their interpreted meaning; his or her resistance to dissociation; and the availability and use of mind-altering substances (including alcohol) also appear capable of affecting the kinds, quantity, and quality of traumatic learning. This in turn can change the way the brain processes things emotionally, which in turn can profoundly change what is associated, interpreted, learned, and remembered. The sheer number of these cofactors that are currently known to affect effective, traumatic learning alone suggests that other systems will soon be added.

THE EXPONENTIAL SUM OF ALL FEAR

Now that the basic learning systems are clearer, I think it's time to summarize traumatic learning as a whole. Traumatic learning can happen "on its own," for example, as a consequence of an earthquake. Traumatic learning, however, is more often initiated, controlled, and almost always affected by a human perpetrator, interlocutor, or teacher. Irrespective of the specific role, fear or intimidation enters the attempt to control, change, or moderate the learner's activities, behaviors, or thoughts. Most often, claims of "teaching" really amount to controlling the victim or student with regard to something the perpetrator, interlocutor, or teacher needs, wants, or desires—usually something they learned traumatically and are reenacting.

Because this form of learning is inexorably imprinted within higher biological organisms at birth, when we survive birth (which all who are reading this have survived), its primacy, power, persistence, and survival value are undeniable. While we quickly repress the birth event, effective traumatic learning is employed whenever we need, want, or desire anything, and it quickly becomes so ubiquitous that it is utilized and reinforced throughout our lives. In fact, we are constantly employing it in various forms with almost everyone we interact with. It is so powerful, effective, and ubiquitous, and we are so blind to it, that the whole shadow world of traumatic learning has become institutionalized in every aspect of our society, including, sadly, our principal hope for change, "teaching" as embodied in our educational system.

PICKING UP THE PIECES

Traumatically learned neurosensory *data*, although fragmentary, are surprisingly persistent and stable. They are the basic elements of traumatic learning. What is learned traumatically doesn't go away—after all, "what was learned was earned," and at a great price. Because what is learned is fragmentary and often misinterpreted, traumatic object-data memory is, in a way, more about triggers than memories: when, how, and in what form they will return when triggered (they always do), and how we will ultimately interpret them in the context of what at this moment seems like a nontraumatic life but clearly isn't. In this sense, we humans live Dr. Jekyll and Mr. Hyde lives. We just don't like to see it, because it is too painful— we live like "walking wounded," constantly alert and afraid of anything that might bring back a cohesive memory of the birth event.

Our propensity towards traumatic learning is not innate—it is a consequence of birth (and perhaps even earlier, prenatal trauma, as for example consciousness awakening) and our inherent neurobiological systems. We have, for example, built into our neural systems two additional learning systems: the sympathetic (neuroelectrical; fast) and neuroendocrine (hormonal; slower) systems, which learn in parallel with the brain's primary learning system and which, at the same time, selectively augment it in traumatic learning situations. It is possible that our sense of reality and unreality comes from the existence and interaction of these multiple, traumatic learning systems. When they agree, what we are learning and eventually learn seem "real" to us; when in conflict, they can seem "really unreal."

Traumatically learned data appear to be somehow clumped together— associated—with other object-data, sensations, and internal feelings, often based on timing—simultaneity, order, and/or rhythmic characteristics. Clinically, order and rhythm seem to create a second set of traumatic object-data that, for all practical purposes, could be expected to be stored in yet another area of the brain, distinct from nonrhythmic neurosensory object-data and neuroelectrical and hormonal sympathetic systems.

Traumatically learned *information*, on the other hand, can change in meaning from within or be changed from outside the learner. Pavlov stated this quite succinctly, from a purely neurophysiologic perspective: "owing to the complexity of . . . the conditioned reflex [it] must, of course, also undergo certain changes, i.e., be constantly corrected" (Pavlov 2001, p. 273). Learners, for example, can be unintentionally or intentionally led into a particular interpretation by another person—a teacher—present at the learning event. Also, learners can themselves unconsciously or consciously, unintentionally or intentionally, spin, distort, or even falsify an existing interpretation, depending on needs, wants, and desires. Third, as interpreted memories are recalled and remembered, they are susceptible to further intentional or unintentional change from within or outside—for example, an interlocutor.

Some respected experts in the area of recall believe that intentional interpretative distortion, notably by either the victim or the victimizer, is so common as to be a hallmark of traumatic learning. In fact, distortion can provide effective, last-ditch "protection" against total neural disintegration during overwhelming traumatic learning events. If you're a "Star Trek" fan, you are saying to yourself, "A-ha! A classical Dr. Spock 'Vulcan conflict' between the rational and the emotional." And isn't intentionally reinterpreting a learning event a lot of what contemporary teaching and education is about?

But based on my clinical experience, there are at least four more factors that strongly influence the degree and effectiveness of traumatic learning: (1) how a learning object is introduced; (2) how the learner experiences the event; (3) the resources available to the learner to interpret the event; and (4) what the event means to the learner's sense of self, society, world, and spirit.

Traditional thinking says that learning, and thereby teaching and education, occurs best when the learner's attention is successfully directed toward a learning object, or when the learning object is repeatedly directed by a teacher or interlocutor into the physical and mental center of the learner's attention. My own clinical experience with traumatic learning suggests, however, that this is not the case at all. In fact, it appears to me to be the opposite.

Traumatic learning acts and events are enacted in a physical, not an ideational, world. It seems reasonable that memory strength and stability would be directly related to the number of times the traumatic act is repeated within a similar context. Clinical observations, however, suggest this is sometimes, but not necessarily always, true (see, for example, the previous example of S.W.).

What I have observed is that repetition invokes two strong but seemingly opposite learning effects. Initially, repetition activates and reinforces the learning process by focusing attention on the central learning act, event, or object. You can demonstrate this if you have a watch on your wrist: Move the watch to a different position on your arm. Your body will begin continuously asking why you moved that watch from a perfectly fine position. But after a minute or two, you'll quit asking yourself and will no longer even notice where the watch is. Your attention will have automatically turned to something else, without your even noticing. In fact, when a particular learning object or event is continually and repetitiously presented, it also creates a rapidly increasing sense of "pressure" to look away and make sure you're not missing anything else. This pressure is quite strong. Not looking away creates a risk of entering into an altered state of consciousness, for example, induced sleep, dissociation, hypnotic trance, or other "frozen" state! And that's equally true for smelling, hearing, tasting, touching, and gut feelings.

My experience is that learning is most effective when the *learner* has to repeatedly bring a peripherally perceived learning object into the center of his or her attention. This takes considerable energy. Conversely, constant focus on a centrally presented learning object that is ultimately not a threat is the fastest way to tire a learner and *make* him or her turn his or her attention elsewhere. In such an instance, any peripheral distraction will suffice, though it's clear from clinical observations that semi-repetitive movement that seems to randomly change, especially high-contrast examples like black and white, loud and soft, or high and low, are more effective.

Try it for yourself: Try keeping your eye constantly on the ball during a long set in a well-matched, professional tennis game. The ball goes back and forth, back and forth. After a few moments, it's so predictable that it becomes hard to keep your eye on the ball, and without noticing, your mind turns to other things: the size of the crowd, a passing cloud, what will be served for dinner tonight. Movies and television work in the same way: Both are really a series of images being constantly refreshed. You can prove this by blinking your eyes quickly as you look at them. But it is extremely difficult to hold on to any one image. Instead, we actually create the illusion of movement—we "see" it. Remember EMDR, mentioned in the section "Music of the Spheres"? It works rather like this, doesn't it?

Even when one focuses tightly on a centrally placed learning object, the object will dissolve when it occurs against learner volition or interest. In such an instance, what is learned will be whatever catches one's senses peripherally—during hypnosis, for example, the words of an interlocutor. This may seem counterintuitive, but I think the longer you consider it, the more instances of effective peripheral learning you will discover.

Do you remember the last nationally televised presidential announcement about the state of our nation? I do—well, vaguely. At least, I remember that I watched it, but what I mainly remember about it is that my wife, in the next room, was talking to a friend about what kind of sushi she was going make for our dinner later!

The power of peripheral learning—that is, the introduction or importance of peripheral learning objects during traumatic fixation—is one of the very reasons that eidetically learned object-data *are* fragmented: During traumatic learning, without even thinking about it, our attention leapfrogs rapidly from one peripheral object to another—a good survival strategy and also a good defense against seeing or feeling in entirety that which one doesn't wish to see or feel happening to oneself against one's will. It has been suggested that "out of body" experiences may originate in this way.

How the learner experiences a traumatic learning event makes all the difference in the world as to not only what is remembered (as in the above instances), but what becomes associated with the learned object-data, and how the whole is interpreted. For example, I recall several World War II veterans describing their war experiences in France. They recalled the war, and how buddy after buddy suddenly ceased to exist, in bitter, horrific terms that contrasted sharply with my father's recollections of the deliciously long fall evenings he spent at Allied headquarters in pleasant conversation with people from all over the world. It was the same war! It's the old case of two blind people describing an elephant. One feels its leg and describes it as a huge, solid, comforting, treelike animal. The other feels its tail and describes it as a thin, sinuous, dangerous, snakelike animal.

Like one's particular experience and point of view, the resources available to the learner at the time of the learning event play a major role in learning, especially with regard to interpretation. A two-year-old, for example, might view violation (e.g., rape) as pleasurable or painful play, a four-year-old as good or evil, a six-year-old as right and wrong choices. Same event, but very different interpretations! Similar traumatic learning events that recur over a period of time would be expected to take on a steadily more complex interpretation, which indeed it seemed to do, for example, in S.W.'s case. Likewise, clinical experience indicates that traumatic learning becomes even more complex—I like to think of it in terms of increasingly rich associative and interpretive meanings—as one "grows up" and develops a consciousness of self, society, world, and spirit.

As we conclude this chapter, recall with me for a moment our first contact in this chapter: alien abductions. Was this case of purported alien abduction "real"? Neurobiologically speaking, the answer must always be yes—both in terms of the victim's and perhaps the perpetrator's needs, wants, and desires surrounding the traumatic learning event (the victim's so that the full impact of violation by a trusted family member can be avoided; the perpetrator's to keep control of the victim and make sure that if anything slips out, it won't be believed). And yes, also, because the perpetrator seemed, and indeed was, alien—at the time of the violation, the perpetrator's behavior was entirely alien to everything the victim knew of "normal" behavior in the "other" world. And remember, it still *could* have been an actual alien abduction in the way we in the "normal" world think of space aliens and UFOs. This would, after all, not be the first, only, or last such claim. Disproving it completely, beyond any shadow of doubt, would be nearly impossible.

And yet I suspect you will still hold on to the belief that it wasn't a "true" alien abduction, in the sense that there was no definitive physical evidence that would force you to dispel all your doubts (is this an unexpected thought in a secret event like this?) and that would carry weight in a courtroom with a judge and jury of peers. Common sense *has* to say it's more likely that such an explanation is wrong. The "truth," whatever it really is, were it known, would be very difficult to accept. What adult hasn't questioned whether, at some time or other, he or she has acted outside the envelope when disciplining a child?

This all leads to the inescapable yet counterintuitive conclusion that things learned at the associative and/or interpretive level—that have acquired a "best" contextual level of meaning, given the various players' needs, wants, and desires—can, in fact, rarely if ever be entirely "true" in the ideal or Platonic sense of ideal truths. More importantly, the whole concept of "teachers teaching truth" should be beginning to uncomfortably unravel! So what's going on here? I think that while teachers are trying to "teach truth," learners are trying to "learn life." There's a fundamental disconnection here. The "learning systems," one traumatic, the other something else, are disconnected. It reminds me of a physician I know who told each of his patients at the end of an office visit the horrors of smoking and strongly urged them to quit smoking—with a cigarette in his hand! Teaching truth—learning life: fundamental disconnection.

But that's not all. In a genuine attempt to "resolve" traumatic learning, most learners seek out similar traumatic learning events in the hope that they will resolve differently. The hope here is that the trauma truly was a freak of nature, something beyond even the hand of God, and "normally" would have played out differently. What usually happens instead is that similar events recruit similar actors and similar outcomes, which ultimately reinforce the trauma. Think *Apocalypse Now*.

The ironic thing about traumatic reenactment is that if it wasn't apocalyptic then, it becomes so now. And it grows increasingly so with each recycling. Clinically speaking, traumatic learners are inclined to seek out and repeat a traumatic learning event to the extent of "voluntary" re-victimization, and in the extreme, victimization of others, if necessary. On the other hand, the converse, that every traumatic learner will inevitably victimize others in the same way they were victimized, has not proven true clinically. Not all effective, traumatic learners are destined to become traumatic teachers! Most, yes. All, no.

And that's still not everything! Based on my clinical observations, it seems to me that traumatized learners resurrect a particular traumatic situation to try to reestablish something fundamental that is broken during traumatic "teaching—learning": I think what is being sought is trust— trust in both a felt and a cognitive sense. So far we have explored three steps, phases, or levels in effective, traumatic learning: eidetic neurosensory data, associations, and interpretations. Trust is different. These three steps, phases, or levels are what trust is built upon—but trust is more. It's somehow tied into consciousness—of ourselves, society, the world as we know it, and spirituality.

The issues discussed in this chapter stretch far beyond data, association, symbolism, and interpretation. Their very existence suggests that traumatic learning must occur on more than just three or four levels. What is missing is how information progresses to knowledge, and how knowledge in turn reunites with the traumatic learning event, giving it further meaning. The result is clearly a new cognizance of a learning event—a sort of "external perspective"—which can then be used as a yardstick to understand the ramifications of what has been learned in the contemporary world. What continues to cut right to the quick of traumatic learning and repressed memory issues is, in fact, the body-mind-spirit continuum. What is yet required to bring effective traumatic learning into balance with a contemporary physical world involves, without a doubt, the difficult issue of trust. Whom should we trust? What and when should we trust? Why must we trust? How, exactly, do we trust?

Chapter Four

Higher Learning

"Just tell me about it," your grandmother might have said. "It'll make you feel better." Who would have thought that Grandma and Freud would agree? Grandma, sometimes with the assistance of oatmeal cookies and milk, was invoking higher—what clinicians call cognitive—learning.

Cognitive learning begins with the conscious restructuring of what has been learned, a consciousness embedded in self-awareness. On the other hand, self-awareness seems to profit from learning, but interestingly, not from all kinds of learning—and especially not traumatic learning. Clinically, self-awareness can be blocked by and often must grow in spite of traumatic learning and teaching. If this is so, then there must exist another form of learning that is effective (self-awareness rarely abandons us) and contributes to a fourth step, phase, or level of learning.

Self-awareness probably begins before birth. My years of work as a pediatrician in the newborn intensive care unit with fetuses as young as twenty weeks since inception suggests that self-awareness probably develops in fetuses well before the normal 36- to 40-week birth event. Perhaps it begins in response to shocks to the system, when the various organs "come online." Perhaps it begins and develops in response to local environmental changes—almost exclusively nonvolitional and thereby traumatic by definition. On the other hand, perhaps it develops in one or more events corresponding to the insufflation of the soul. Self-awareness might also be "taught" to parent(s); as fetuses attempt to make their needs, wants, and desires known, their definition of self and awareness might develop based on chemical or even perceived neurosensory responses. I have often wondered whether the first mode of human communication might not be purely chemical. But whatever mode it takes, the earliest learning would be highly effective, if only because it's being based on "casino" rules: What is needed, wanted, or desired is occasionally but not regularly and predictably met, and when met, may be so in ways different from those expected. I have come to believe that it is one or a combination of these learning situations that drives fetal self-awareness into being.

At birth—our personal "Big Bang"—whatever self-awareness was present is probably at least temporarily suppressed. Later on it may be reinitiated through magic, astrology, Ouija boards, *National Enquirer* stories, or other forms of "casino" learning—what one of my colleagues ventured to call "willing traumas." But the sad truth is that while this process is going on, we rarely touch or even acknowledge the underlying trauma and neurobiology that is constantly at work.

Given what little we actually know about where it comes from in any particular situation, cognitive learning does seem to begin with a learning event or act, often traumatic, and typically advances on through some further stages such as emotion, global meaning, and finally recontextualization, resulting in the reorganization and probably reconnection of all the learning steps, phases, or levels. For example, cognitive relearning is an important weapon in my clinical arsenal for resolving the effects of trauma. But whatever I think of its advantages toward overcoming something unwanted that was traumatically learned, or as a tool to help prepare for an arduous exam, it's no good unless a learner determines to use it. This tool goes by common names, and in many common forms; whether fables, myths, archetypes, or "New Age" homilies, they still work. What makes them work is a learner's personal ability to generalize and adhere to them: further evidence of the body-mind-spirit at work and play.

In 1890 Freud independently acknowledged that at least some unwanted thoughts and behaviors, as well as associated feelings, could be alleviated if in the process of recall the object-data fragments could be "put into words." Further studies during and after World War II, however, left Freudian psychoanalysts working with trauma victims convinced that the verbal unburdening of traumatic memories was not in itself sufficient to effect a lasting cure. Instead, unwanted, traumatically learned feelings and behaviors seemed to be periodically revisited—in a similar manner if there was little recovery, and in a different manner if there was sufficient recovery. It was as if one was being given the chance of reworking the trauma—reworking areas that were ineffectively resolved during the last revisitation, and then at progressively higher steps, phases, or levels.

What was missing, the clinical evidence began to show in case after case, was something to touch and affect the cognitive learning processes as well. Although trauma often robs the learner of a way to fully articulate the crisis within, the mind races ahead to seek out all possible ways to call for help. Deliberate, cognitive expression, whether in the form of drawings, sand play, music, touch, or a new recovery language, can mediate the internal battles. But while the lines are easily drawn, they are also constantly shifting . . . how then does one acquire something he or she doesn't have? How does one articulate needs across entirely different worlds? Perhaps the question then is not when, but where and how self-awareness begins.

SELF MEETS SELF

During recovery from trauma, cognitive reawakening begins with the formation of a close bond with another person(s). But it can't be a teacher-student bond. Recovery isn't about knowing when or how, but doing—trusting—and getting unmet needs met. If this sounds a bit mystical or Zenlike, I apologize. It does, however, represent a fundamental shift from traumatic teaching to supported self-learning. I know survivors who know more about therapy than I do. Some were in therapy before I graduated from elementary school. Yet, though they know exactly what needs to be done, they don't do it. They hesitate casting themselves back out into that sea of experience. Why?

Actually, I have found over the years that learners—survivors—pretty much *know what they need*. They also seem to know what resources they need to surround themselves with before it's reasonably safe to cognitively reawaken themselves. What's usually missing is secure surroundings, free of perpetrators *and teachers*. Sometimes that translates to having adequate finances, sometimes to being in a position of power and control over feelings. But most important is the presence of a mentor—someone who is not a teacher with his or her own agenda, but is a real, live, observable, testable, self-aware human being who can demonstrate self-awareness. Remember my medical colleague who was trying to help his patients quit smoking?

What they needed wasn't a lesson on what to do, but a doctor who could model doing it—quitting, or not smoking altogether. I call this new kind of "teacher" a mentor. A mentor doesn't always have to know how to do it—but he or she must be willing to do it, and to let the learner observe the process. What process? Trust. Trust that out of the mere effort will come something—the cry for help will be rewarded.

It doesn't even have to actually work (fix, resolve, succeed, win). When effort (and thereby trust) is demonstrated, mentoring works. Unlike a teacher, a mentor can fail in front of learners, because mentoring is not strictly about knowing, fixing, resolving, succeeding, or winning—it's about persevering and trusting. And in case you're already leaping ahead, yes, there is more to mentoring than just persevering and trusting, but that's how it starts, and that's where self-awareness or self-reawareness— waking up, coming out of one's shell, getting on with life, and cognitive learning—rebegins.

YOUR PLACE, MY SPACE

Mentoring as I describe it is an incredible, awesome, awe-inspiring responsibility, one that few classically trained teachers can do or tolerate. The mentor, model, or imprinteur is something other than an interlocutor, interrogator, or teacher. He or she may serve as a mentor for a short time or over a lifetime, for one or many different learning events or acts. During most traumatic learning events or acts, what is significant is the lack of a mentor: the learner is left alone, isolated. Recall for a moment how you felt in many of your formal, institutional education classes.

Students are repetitively told what to do, compelled to act or behave in a particular way, and in the end tested to see if they have acquired the "correct" information from the teacher. By virtue of being a teacher, and to limit the extent of the trauma, students are kept at a "safe" distance. Teachers encourage students to "do what I say"—to focus on the ideal— and not study a teacher's human foibles. If students don't want to learn what is centrally presented, teachers use "teaching tricks" like making the topic into a game or entertaining the students.

If you find this hard to believe, attend any postgraduate teachers' meeting: What is most sought are "new teaching techniques." The trouble with tricking students is that it does not lead to trust. It turns into the ultimate betrayal. Teaching and traumatic learning are actually a constant reenactment of betrayal, whether it is the teacher or student breaking trust. Like trauma, it's hard to "see" how ubiquitous and damaging the teaching really is.

The importance of the mentor role in learning is difficult to overstate. When asked what it was during recovery that helped the most, several survivors immediately blurted out, "You!"

We are born in, surrounded by, and immersed in trauma and traumatic learning. It's truly amazing to me that we can step outside our universe and see the importance of mentorship—even more, what makes a mentor a mentor. Mentorship is not new. I often say that it formally began over 2400 years ago, with the great philosopher and mentor Socrates. It also formally ended over 2300 years ago, with Socrates' pupil, the incredibly effective teacher Plato.

Nor has mentorship gone unstudied. For a while, much of the psychological world focused its formidable research abilities on one or another aspect of mentoring—for example, imprinting in animals and humans. It hasn't gone entirely unrecognized, either. In the 1930s the National Socialist Party in Germany made extensive use of mentoring to legitimize what we now recognize as a particularly effective learning technique called propagandizing and brainwashing.

Mentorship is in some ways an opposite of teaching. For example, teachers must be in control of their class. Entire curricula and educational efforts are directed toward teaching teachers classroom management. Mentorship requires one to let go of control and dictation of information, as well as "truth" to disciples. In a sense, the first role of a mentor may even be pejorative. For example, I have repeatedly noticed that learners inculcated in traumatic learning often have great difficulty letting go of it. After all, it is so familiar, and most survivors I have known yearn so strongly for the illusion that they have obtained some mastery over it, that they become willing to do almost anything for it. If this seems hard to understand, imagine for just a moment how vulnerable you actually are in this world. Uncomfortable, isn't it?

I recall an exercise in a public health class in which we were asked to try to comprehend how much suffering there was in the world. It began with a rather formal recitation of statistics on war, poverty, hunger, crime, and misery. It was so uncomfortable that one student began vomiting, and the exercise had to be terminated early. But we all got the point. One of my fellow students pointed out after class that this realization, if maintained for longer than a few moments, could drive one to suicide.

If most educators are lost in their teaching, then where can one find an example of a mentor? Interestingly, when I look with my eyes wide open, I have observed barbers, hairstylists, small-town grocers, and even bartenders mentoring. I have read about and listened to national sports heroes struggle with whether they should mentor or teach.

Just as there are many different kinds of teachers, maybe as many as there are individual teachers, are there also different kinds of mentors? I believe so. I have watched in awe as rock superstars like Alice Cooper and Michael Jackson attempt to both teach through overwhelming spectacle and mentor through demonstration during live rock concerts. What exactly are they teaching and mentoring? Feeling uncomfortable again?

In my previous book I began to explore in detail a specific form of mentoring I call *emendative* mentoring ("reflective" might be a more familiar term), like that accomplished by a good therapist, tutor, or adviser. There are probably other forms, for example, enriching (e.g., an enlightened mentor with extensive experiential resources—a licensed massage therapist, or a co-survivor) or observational (as in a traditional Freudian psychotherapist or someone witnessing another person's recovery). I don't claim to know all the different kinds of mentors at this point, but I have observed that mentorship can take various forms employing different methods and techniques.

Irrespective of type, the result of mentoring is a stepwise, conscious resculpting by the learner of his or her own conscious ideas about a learning event . . . and thereby of the learner's self. In this step, phase, or level, learners make awesome choices from among intensely personal (and as we've seen in examples including alien abductions) incredibly rich, highly symbolic body-mind-spirit associations. Piaget and gestalt psychologists called these choices "thought adaptation" and "transposition." These terms suggest but don't fully indicate the immense amount of energy and burden borne by some learners during cognitive awakening or reawakening, learning or relearning. Teachers actually add to this burden or, at the least, constantly get in the way. Only a mentor can help carry the weight. Only a mentor can demonstrate the trust that is necessary for true, volitional learning to begin to take place. Mentorship is, however, more than just not getting in the way. At the least, it is not getting into the learner's space.

Teaching requires the teacher to get into the learner's space and exert control over the confusion; as some linguistic colleagues would say, "tidying up someone else's intellectual mess." It requires that the teacher's "correct" thoughts—ideals—be exactly conveyed, without change (after all, they are ideal), to replace a learner's "childish" or "incorrect" thoughts. Teachers need to both understand and manipulate what a learner is learning.

Mentorship does not involve taking one person's ideas and carefully inserting them into another's brain. Mentorship involves demonstrating one's own process of learning in parallel with the learner. Mentor and student do not necessarily have to be learning the same thing, or even be working on the same learning act or event. But they do need to be learning—processing—somewhat in parallel. A mentor shows students how he or she is learning and demonstrates trust in both his or her own and the student's learning process.

One classical measure of teaching is that learning should get easier with practice. In fact, students become more and more dependent on the teacher to tell them what to think. What actually becomes easier is the teacher's teaching, not the learner's ability to learn. Students must learn to trust a teacher, whether it is justified or not. One of the most difficult concepts for many of my international students, for example, is learning not to believe everything their teacher says or they read in textbooks. Insightful questioning places the teacher and his or her ideals "on trial." This conflicts with the very notion of critical, independent thinking. As I said, at best a good teacher gets in the way. At worst the learner eventually regresses back into being a docile child. No questions. No hassles. Obedient. A quiet, orderly classroom filled with quiet, orderly, "model" students.

The most important measure of learning is that a learner can learn independently without invoking the myriad problems that accompany teaching and violational learning. With good mentorship, *nothing becomes easier*. Instead, what is learned by demonstration is that irrespective of experience, nontraumatic learning always takes effort. It is difficult, demanding, and exhausting. Students learn to trust that learning will inevitably result from their own efforts and that it will be effective—that one doesn't need to invoke traumatic learning! Everything can be and is questioned, because the teacher is not on trial here—rather, both mentor and student are each seeking their own truth.

Mentorship directly supports independent, critical listening, reading, writing, and thinking. The mentor doesn't get in the way; his or her ideas simply become irrelevant. Learners learn, through observing mentors in the act of learning, that the disquieting feelings that arise before making a discovery are "normal" and not a sign of weakness, inexperience, lack of effort, or incompetence.

Mentored learners become *individually* empowered. Questions lead to more questions, until they begin flying about everywhere. Hassles—frustrations—build as learners delve deeper and deeper into the issue. To an observer, mentored classrooms seem uncontrolled, unmanaged, and sometimes, as the tension builds, chaotic. A good mentor receives respect, not for his or her teaching skills, but for providing a rich learning environment. I have had highly educated teacher-observers say to me that there really is no classroom; rather, everyone seems to be "doing their own thing." Oddly, with less outside control learners seem to pace *themselves* in a roughly parallel manner!

More importantly, there is something special that results from trust acquired through mentorship without teaching: Individual curiosity becomes honored, cherished, cultivated, and expressed, and soon flourishes. American educators seem to especially pride themselves in stating that acquiring the ability to think critically and independently is the very heart and soul of baccalaureate (college) education. Yet in virtually the same breath, if there is one complaint that I uniformly hear from teachers—from preschool to postgraduate educators, and even from good "teacher"-style therapists—it is that in spite of their best efforts, the "better" their students learn, the more curiosity, the very lifeblood of critical thinking, seems to be driven from them. If there is one indictment of our current educational system, from beginning to end, that I believe is truly deserved, it is that no matter how much money and effort are poured into it, better teaching cannot and will not help learners become better critical thinkers (one reviewer's comment: "Why wasn't I taught mentoring in my educator training program!?").

RIPPLES IN THE POND OF CONSCIOUSNESS

During the days of the repressive military junta in Brazil, a former director of Libertad prison, a "political" prison that used trauma to interrogate and rehabilitate prisoners, reputedly said, "[O]ne day we'll have to let them go, so we'll have to take advantage of the time we have left to drive them mad" (Weschler 1998, p. 131). To me, this statement sounds like something out of George Orwell's futuristic novel *1984*, but 1984 is already past, and I've heard this kind of statement in one form or another repeated on one television soap after another, and in movie after movie—it isn't so shocking anymore. I've even heard it said at parties that it's all just another version of Andy Warhol's famous fifteen-minute pop edict: None of us knows when we'll get our fifteen minutes of attention from society.

Actually, the above strongly suggests that there's more to this fourth step, phase, or level of learning than one person's consciousness. For the moment, I would like to call this "bigger than any one learner's cognition" *metacognition*, and define it as a sweeping interplay of collective consciousness. I've observed in trauma recovery that everything learned will eventually develop a social, world, and spiritual meaning. The steps, phases, or levels of learning involved in this process are constantly going on whether we like it or not.

In the best of circumstances, metacognition means a learner can change at least the meaning of his or her traumatic memories, and thereby the world. Learners are not powerless. Unfortunately, it also affords teaching and teachers further opportunities to interfere with our individual discovery process, much in the same way that the former director of the Libertad prison was planning to do. True, there is a sense of draconian malevolence present in the latter and, we hope instead, a sense of loving-kindness in our school teachers. Yet given the ubiquitous nature of trauma, I wonder . . . Torture is an extreme example of traumatic teaching—but still teaching, nonetheless. In this particular case, it involved an attempt to stamp out meaningful memory of what had been done and, in the end, manipulate the very soul. The torture described above employed metacognition (the learner was taught that he or she "brought it on him- or herself"), in an attempt to change the recollection of what actually happened (assault and battery). But irrespective of intent—whether from kindness, affection, and love, or from sadism, dislike, and hate, teaching and traumatic learning eventually invoke metacognition, and metacognition is a singularly powerful element of learning . . . in general terms, it makes what was learned liberating or enslaving.

To make therapy most effective, one must eventually affect a fundamental, conscious learning "transformation." When Grandma said that "telling" is good for you, she was inviting you to consciously transform what was bothering you into something that would instead recreate space for your creativity, open a channel for discovery, and ultimately liberate your soul. But it's not just retelling—it's retelling it to a trusted mentor, not teacher, who *by example* demonstrates metacognition. Metacognition requires a different language, rich in symbols, grounded in the body and "gut feeling."

Symbolism is a fundamental part of metacognition. Pavlov once described symbolic metacognition as a volitional, conditioned associative process. Since Pavlov's early work, he has been repeatedly criticized for relying too strictly on automatic, autonomic, even mindlessly symbolic cognition. To some extent, I agree. I also think that much of the criticism is misplaced: We have a lot more information about learning and, more importantly, about how the brain functions during learning, than Pavlov had at his disposal. The reason I hesitate to simply dismiss Pavlov is because, as Pavlov showed, teaching in its most brutal form can be used to reduce memory to stimulus and drool. If we must acknowledge but apply with caution Pavlov's findings, we must be even more cautious with Freud.

Metacognitive learning extends well beyond what Freud called the self, or "ego." Metacognition implies a conscious and integrated, personal "inner self"—a consciousness of the consciousness of self—fitting within societal, world, and spiritual contexts. Metacognition requires not just consciousness, but also meaning, and thereby trust in and a valuing of the inner self.

For most people, metacognition "makes sense" but remains difficult to grasp, especially when one talks of social, world, and spiritual metacognition without including the actual experiencing of it. And while I don't want to try to teach it to you (that would make me a teacher), perhaps I can demonstrate it, in a mentoring sense, even over time and distance. Here's an experience that I had during my days as a research associate with the United States National Academy of Science, assigned to the United States National Aeronautics and Space Administration (NASA) international space station effort: While studying various space station analogs, I ran across a book called *Biosphere* by Vladimir Vernadsky, an eminent twentieth-century Russian scientist who wrote of a "noetic" metacognitive awakening in which humans suddenly become aware of themselves as a living element of Earth's biosphere—a living entity deeply affected by its elements (us) and yet at the same time, constantly and collectively affecting them all. Substitute Earth for biosphere and you have Gaia, the living planet. In his book *To Rule the Night*, former NASA astronaut James Irwin said, "As we flew into space we had a new sense of ourselves, of the earth, and of the nearness of God. I sensed the beginning of some sort of deep change taking place inside of me."

While I have never personally been into space, I have experienced "zero gravity" six miles high, on NASA's "Vomit Comet." Two nights after flying my experiment, I began to vividly and quite pleasantly reexperience the sensation of free fall in my dreams. These dreams were very rich and transformative—I suddenly began seeing Earth as a tiny spinning ball locked into an eternal free fall in the vastness of space. I viewed Earth differently. Somehow it was more personal, more fragile—I felt that I was an extension of it, and it was an extension of me. To this day, I *feel in my "gut"* that I am a living part of it and it is a part of me. I am now aware that my very life depends wholly on it, and its future depends upon me. These days, when asked if I could add one educational experience to our educational system that I would promote transformative discovery of, and an understanding of its place in education, I seriously suggest an optional microgravity or spaceflight experience, much like a summer visit to Greece after completing the junior year of college.

Darwin might scratch his head over this rather unorthodox point of view, and yes, there are disagreements about the nature and the limits of metacognition. Exactly where symbolic understanding ends and metacognitive learning begins, as well as where exactly the boundaries of self, society, world, and spirit begin and end, are not entirely clear. To me, at this point in my own journey, they seem to overlap, and that doesn't cause me problems. On the other hand, some have pointed out that marital, social, and work problems do not immediately or ultimately always improve with therapy (they *should*, if therapy completely and effectively "fixes" traumatic learning). It's clear to me that it's important to do more than just learn to speak the unspeakable, tell one's story, and then figure out how everything went wrong. There needs to be a mentor with an oatmeal cookie somewhere there too.

World and spiritual metacognition can be difficult to grasp, and when grasped do not assure a mental hold for any duration other than the moment. Still, I would like to mention a few observations about each: In my experience, world metacognition is surprisingly visible in the recovery process. Work, money, and power are widely considered to be three traditional areas of cognitive recovery. Together these translate into personal, social, world, and spiritual metacognition.

I have observed many survivors and other learners go through these stages, phases, or levels of learning, but one especially stands out in my mind: F.H., a 40-year-old female who was assaulted and battered repeatedly—physically, sexually, emotionally, and psychologically—from roughly six to over eighteen years of age. She came from a family of political activists, and much of the abuse was justified within this context. I had the privilege of witnessing her slow but successful struggle to regain a political identity of her own.

The high point of this process for me was her discovery that her identity within the world was in fact different from and not controlled by her family's political justification of the abuse. In reality, only in the Greek "body politic" (where *polis* refers to small groups of free citizens efficiently engaged in the making of policy) does world identity come close to world metacognition. World metacognition is not so much a physical situation or arrangement, as a *felt* sense—a point of view sensed internally in the visceral "gut"—about how one fits into the world outside the traumatic learning events.

Similarly, spirituality does not mean religion. By religion, I mean a club or cult—a group of interested people meeting together to practice or act out rituals. By spiritual, I mean some kind of a personalized relationship to a higher power. I have had the privilege of seeing a wide range of spirituality, from transformative spiritual "rebirth" (for example, a "born-again" Christian), to the "force" being with you, to realization of one's personal destiny. The spiritual form is not as important as the need for it to be a personal relationship between the learner and a power greater than one's own physical body.

Metacognitive learning is about relearning "meaning" in an ever-widening spiral of internal to external contexts. It represents the last stages of acquisition of the new language necessary to speak what could not be spoken in the very broadest sense. Another way to look at it is that metacognition is not necessarily about developing a new dictionary—that happens in the first three steps, phases, or levels—but at this point, a new thesaurus. It is not so much the definitions and associations of object-data that change as what, taken together, they mean in individual, social, world, and spiritual contexts.

Clinically, metacognition has the power to realign previously blocked associations and relationships and, once initiated, spirals outwards, like ripples in a pond, affecting not only the learner but virtually anyone in contact with the learner. Learners, witnesses, mentors, and contacts alike are often shaken with sudden insights of their own, and like earthquake aftershocks, they continue to occur for weeks, months, and even years afterward.

When individual metacognition occurs and sets off a tsunami of metacognition, that ripple in time affords society, the world, and perhaps even our higher power the chance to learn, as if it too had a physical life of its own. That's a staggering claim, but consider for a moment Martin Luther King Jr.'s "I Had a Dream" speech and how it challenged an entire nation to revisit the meaning of individual freedom. Women's rights, same-sex partnerships—whether you like them or not—are collective, metacognitive ripples moving right now through our society, the world, and the collective human spirit. They are creating, in essence, a circular spiral—time's own rhythm—where the "now" becomes another opportunity to revisit and relearn what we have discovered at yet another level. The "silent majority," in this sense, is anything but silent! We are a traumatized society, steeped in our own traumatic past, our individual traumas, wearing traumatic blinders. My hope is that the next metacognitive storm to thunder though our society, world, and spirit will be that of mentored, nonviolational learning, and that with it will come a freedom the likes of which our world has never known—freedom from the shackles of traumatic learning.

Is there is a "new world order" in the air? I prefer to ask whether we are individually and collectively ready to face our traumatic past and burdens and allow ourselves to evolve to a new form of learning, freedom, and understanding.

POSTCARDS FROM THE UNCONSCIOUS

Traumatic memories are more than links between the learner and the contemporary world. They literally enmesh learner, memories, and recall within physical reality. The place of intersection, the learning nexus, is our senses.

Sensations come from zillions of intricate *physical* neural networks that create a unique mesh of *ephemeral* electrical impulses—and these are what make us unique. Add the ability to abstract or symbolize and a strong proclivity toward rhythm and musicality, all of which evoke similar neurosympathetically and hormonally mediated reflexes, to which we react surprisingly similarly, and we have a balanced critical mass sufficient for the beginnings of interpersonal communication.

Common factors such as these create within us a sense of *anticipation*—knowing (not just guessing) what conditioned motor or visceral response should and will result from a particular stimulus. Many of the popular issues of this century seem to me to be the pitting of anticipated outcome, based on one's view of the past, against actualized future outcome. Where anticipation, outcome, and the learner's personal needs, wants, and desires intersect, a felt sense of *justice* emerges. Notice I said justice, not revenge.

In the early 1940s a German researcher named Konrad Lorenz, in an article entitled "Die angeborener Formen möglicher Erfahrung" [Innate Forms of Possible Experience] in the German journal *Zeitschrift für Tierpsychologie*, identified and later successfully demonstrated the application of an aspect of metacognitive learning he called *Weltanschauung*. Weltanschauung is a restructured worldview based on a conscious reinterpretation of something learned. Lorenz's work, undoubtedly brilliant, was noticed by the German Nazi Party, and was subsequently both ruthlessly and efficiently applied.

THE DARKER SIDE OF THE MOON

Lorenz's ideas were incorporated into the Nazis' German national education effort immediately prior to and during World War II. While our contemporary world reluctantly acknowledges his work, probably because of the traumatic context within which it was applied, versions of it persist in terms of the gestalt movement and modern propaganda. "Gestalt" literally refers to a summed-up shape, social configuration, arrangement, or organization. I'm using gestalt a little differently here to refer to consciously selected, collective, associative, symbolic, and metacognitive components of effective learning, whether violational (traumatic) or volitional (nontraumatic). Gestalt psychology and philosophy, presenting as it does a cohesive worldview, is often perceived as the ultimate in world metacognition. It is, however, in the application—the context—that Lorenz's work, gestalt, and other forms of metacognitive learning become "dark" or "light." The mere existence and recognition of metacognitive learning in its various steps, phases, or levels does not in any way guarantee how it will be used. It is in fact the respective teacher or mentor who largely decides this.

To many, worldview—world metacognition—appears strongly resistant to change. An individual's point of view, within the context of a particular political or cultural system of beliefs (especially in our modern, often highly propagandized times), may seem so resistant as to be viewed as transformationally "hopeless." I have always felt otherwise: Therapeutic approaches aimed specifically at changing an individual's world metacognition can become frankly unethical. I can neither support nor espouse their use, although, in shades of Joseph Mengele, they have and will continue to provide a pathway, albeit a very dark one, to understanding metacognition.

Consider for a moment electroconvulsive therapy (ECT), a "contemporary" form of treatment designed to loosen or destroy cognitive linkages, including sometimes a world point of view. ECT effectively destroys cognitive links in addition to social, personal, symbolic, interpretive, associative, and object-data linkages, and unfortunately, it does it indiscriminatively. While ECT may be initiated volitionally, because the process itself is indiscriminative and often offered as a "last-resort" measure, it is a hot ethical question as to whether the "informed consent" required is indeed informed or volitional. Many would argue that it's like signing a blank check for unspecified products for a similarly unspecified amount. Worse yet, the trauma of the treatment carries with it all the liabilities of traumatic learning!

We all suffer to some extent from the effects of trauma. I don't know about you, but the image of pay-as-you-go ECT relearning centers is just too Orwellian for me to want to envision. Similarly, "chemically man-aged" learning, despite its appeal to convenience, seems equally dark to me. On the other hand, I don't want you to get the idea that I am against medication, or that I champion abandoning all medication. I'm a physi-cian; medications have their place. If I have high blood pressure, I'd gladly take medication over a stroke! Used judiciously, medication can help a survivor rediscover the kinesthetic feeling of joy or a good night's sleep without constantly intrusive nightmares. But medications don't fix schools or trauma—at least, not yet. I reiterate: Learners know what they need, and that is to find a metacognitive perception of the trauma that will work for them in the contemporary physical world.

Faith and trust are inherent elements of effective cognitive learning, whether the learning process is volitional or violational, and they eventu-ally lead to a personal understanding of "truth." It is interesting to me that we struggle hard to keep our "truths" consistent with our experience of in-ternal time consciousness: That is, tightly held truths generally fit our ex-perience of ordered linearity: from past to present, from data to associa-tions, to symbolism, to self-awareness, and to social, world, and spiritual meaning.

Interestingly, survivors have often commented to me that memories at the pre-self-awareness level "feel" different than cognitive memories, to the point that the latter are often referred to collectively as "knowledge" rather than memories. In a similar manner, some have consistently voiced an internal, physically felt distinction between knowledge, as defined here, and faith, trust, and truth, which collectively I call "wisdom."

Just as impressive as the existence of *felt* truth and wisdom is the strong human proclivity to interpret memories in relation to the developmental stage. A child, for example, will cognitively interpret data, associations, and symbols differently than an adult at a different developmental stage with more experiences and memories. The nature of the truths that a learner holds surrounding any particular learning event provides clues as to when in one's physical, mental, and spiritual development the learning event occurred. Interesting . . . and yet I have seen it demonstrated many times that learning is more than just different things learned at different developmental stages—learner interaction with the mentor, and the re-sulting *felt* sense of truth and wisdom, are what ultimately make what is learned *real*.

I am frequently surprised at how often and with what ease survivors and learners alike can simultaneously hold multiple, mutually exclusive interpretations, truths, or wisdom. This, more than anything else, separates teaching (the attempted instillation of Platonic ideals) from learning (making sense of neurosensory experiences surrounding a learning event or act). This incredible, distinctly human ability suggests to me that cognitive learning might not actually occur linearly, but in fact may result from recursive renditions of—returns to—the trauma. I imagine this figuratively as a central dot—the centralized object-data—surrounded by a cloud of associations out of which project a potentially infinite number of rays of learning. These rays represent cognitive knowledge, truths, and wisdom. They are not parallel—at least not in the strict sense. They radiate out from a common center, becoming increasingly divergent. In this sense, the embedding in memory of something learned is infinitely plastic, but in an unusual way: Knowledge, truths, and wisdom are based on eidetic commonalities, but they can easily accommodate and even wholly incorporate multiple, mutually exclusive truths and wisdom. Another variant of this is that what we accept as individual, societal, world, or spiritual truth can be, and often is, simultaneously rejected as personal truth. Where attempts to unify and reconcile broader social, world, or spiritual issues are in conflict, cults based on beliefs often assert themselves.

I have come to define a cult as the collective persons and rituals associated with a set of beliefs surrounding an object of worship or veneration. Cults take many forms. In general, most religions (not faith, mind you, but religions) are, by definition, cults. Catholics have held in the past that Protestantism is a cult, and Protestants sometimes insist that Catholicism is cultish. Cults may be based on individual, social, world, and/or spiritual interpretations of what is learned. Some, like vegetarianism, seem innocuous enough and can even be fun—others, like anti-Semitism, can be hellishly destructive for both victims and perpetrators. When present or interjected into learning events, cultism can be frighteningly traumatic, and the repercussions vast and seemingly unresolvable.

This, however, is not a book about cultism and exorcism. The neurobiological importance of cultism is that, first, it is not the same as spirituality, and second, when present or invoked, it is incredibly effective at crystallizing broad collections of learned data and information—even across a number of learning acts—into long-term traumatic memory.

Metacognitive steps, phases, or levels of learning, unlike data, associations, interpretations, and symbols (from which they emerge), and ideational beliefs (which one holds), create strong affectations within an individual's contemporary sense of being—personality. While truth is said to be the highest ideal of teaching, ideal truth simply does not exist neurobiologically. Teaching imparts ritualized beliefs. On the other hand, the highest step, phase, or level of neurobiological learning that we have discussed so far is wisdom. Wisdom cannot be effectively imparted through ideas or ideals—it is imparted through repetitive demonstration or mentorship, acquired through the senses, and cognitively integrated into each memory through repetition and consistent positive reinforcement.

A SUNDIAL IN THE SHADE

While our understanding of traumatic learning as a model for effective learning is quite new, many distinguished physicians, scientists, educators, and linguists have picked away at the Gordian knot and carefully described some of the various threads that seem to run through effective learning. For the moment, we will continue to focus our attention on important but representative clinical studies in humans.

In 1955, scientist-psychologist-educator Emmy Werner and clinical psychologist Ruth Smith began a long-term study that will, I believe, continue to be recognized as one of the most important field studies on traumatic learning and its outcomes. The first results began to be published around 1970, and they continue to be a work in progress. Even if the topic is daunting, you'll enjoy it: This part of our investigation takes us back to the Garden Island, beautiful Kauai, Hawaii—at that time, a sleepy, quiet island where it could be said that everyone pretty much knew everyone and what they were doing. Werner and Smith enlisted every pregnant woman on the island, following, and where that was impossible, accounting for every resulting birth through adulthood today.

In the first book, *The Children of Kauai*, Werner described low-, medium-, and high-risk pregnancy outcomes, providing rich physical, developmental, and behavioral data on children subject to perinatal stress. In the second book, *Kauai's Children Come of Age*, Werner and Smith described persistent physical and behavioral problems in perinatal trauma survivors throughout childhood that were highly resistant to change including directed intervention. Their observations on the outcome of trauma and traumatic learning led some to postulate that survivors might suffer from permanently damaged or defective brains.

Over the years this idea grew in popularity, to the point that Dr. Bessel van der Kolk, a physician working with abused children and adults abused as children, postulated in his groundbreaking book *Psychological Trauma* that these changes were both anatomical and biochemical. If the results of trauma and traumatic learning lead to anatomically defective brains, then, the argument goes, retraining could not be expected to work. In fact, van der Kolk's work has helped identify and clarify many of the basic neurobiological elements involved in traumatic learning.

In her most recent work, "The Children of Kauai: Resiliency and Recovery in Adolescence and Adulthood," published in the *Journal of Adolescent Health* in 1992, Werner describes a different long-term outcome: While it was true that two-thirds of the high-risk children developed problems, one-third did not, and these grew into competent adults without the need for external intervention. More surprising, most of the two-thirds who had significant problems as children and teenagers had also become competent adults by the time they reached their thirties. One factor attributed to those who recovered was the *presence of a significant mentor.*

Consider now the eminent scientist, child psychologist, and educator Jean Piaget, who in lectures and in his now-famous books *Child's Conception of the World*, *The Psychology of the Child*, and *The Language and Thought of the Child* identified distinct stages of development and often intensive activity, separated by quiet periods of what he called information and processing reorganization in children.

Piaget acknowledged that birth was a traumatic learning event. From birth to about seven months of age, an infant gains some control of muscles and becomes able to sort sensations from motor actions. From eight to ten months of age, infants are absorbed in identifying and integrating feelings; this is followed by a period from ten months to two years of age devoted to neurological sensorimotor-feeling integration. During this third period, at about twelve months of age, most begin to demonstrate coarse symbolic-level speaking.

From two to seven years, children become engrossed in the assimilation of symbols and their expression in the form of signs such as numbers, numeric operations, words, and sentences. Between the third and sixth years, two particularly unusual phenomena occur that begin to distinguish the human child from other animals: There is a sudden burst in speed and integration in select neurosensory and neuromuscular systems, and the earliest, rudimentary sense of awareness develops. From seven to eleven years of age, the child practices utilizing mathematical and linguistic symbols. At around ten years of age, a sense of "reflective intelligence" awakens, followed from eleven to fifteen years of age by a period of interest in establishing separate and coordinated individual and social identities.

The famous physician-educator Maria Montessori, in her seminal book *The Secret of Childhood*, also acknowledged the primacy of birth as the first traumatic event. She describes "sensitive" periods during which the senses seem to awaken and guide the development reflex, and motor, psychic, rhythmic, ordinal, symbolic, kinetic, intellectual, cognitive, and devotional behavior.

The once highly controversial psychologist Diane McGuinness, in her brilliant book *When Children Don't Learn*, approached learning from the perspective of learning disability. In the course of her clinical studies, she questioned and ultimately rejected the "brain damage" hypothesis in most cases, in favor of sex differences in the developing-organizing brain, style of sensorimotor integration, interest, and ultimately learning.

Werner, van der Kolk, Piaget, Montessori, and McGuinness, to name just a few of the more recent contributors to what I collectively call the German school of neurobiological learning, all refer to ordered, sensitive, developmental periods of effective learning that collectively correspond to the components, phases, or steps of traumatic learning!

With this firmly in mind, it's time to turn our attention to a particularly important and knotty aspect of learning: intelligence. Piaget's firsthand observations on childhood development, mentioned above, led to the establishment of a system for predicting a "developmental" age distinct from physical age. From this new perspective, I would like to explore intelligence and its relationship to effective learning.

A LITTLE MATTER OF SEX

The great pioneers of trauma, epitomized by the physicians Jean-Martin Charcot and Sigmund Freud, made public an observation that was not only socially disturbing, but also seemed almost heretical in a then male-dominated, patristic society: Sexual abuse victims were more often female and, when uncovered, sexual perpetrators were more often male. This unfortunately fit with the growing body of information about the male hormone and its effect on both males and females.

In my clinical practice, however, this information puzzled me. As a clinician from the 1960s to the turn of the century, I was seeing almost equal numbers of female and male trauma survivors. In addition, the medical, educational, psychological, and learning-disability literature was beginning to agree that while some were struggling mightily to get societies to recognize and begin to erase this gender inequity, the rest of the world was just awakening to how pervasive, important, and profound sexualized trauma really was.

True, trauma survivors as a broad group might be expected to be more gender equitable than sexual abuse survivors, but interestingly, most of the males I was working with eventually discovered that they were sexual abuse survivors. It is also true that clinical observations are notorious with regard to population bias—after all, people pick a particular clinician based on individual needs. But there were growing numbers of reports that suggested that in reality, childhood abuse, even when sexualized, or perhaps more correctly sexually ritualized, was more an act of violation than sex. Even so, it started me questioning: How is gender related to effective learning? And if intelligence is truly a measure of aptitude to learn, does gender truly affect our capacity to learn?

Intelligence has proven a slippery concept whether in clinical, classroom, or laboratory settings. Most people acquire developmental skills—that is, become more skilled and knowledgeable as they age, and by definition, most quantitative measures of intelligence must, to some extent at least, measure current skills, knowledge, abilities, and the attainment of developmental milestones. In addition, intelligence as envisioned by Piaget and later developed by the French educator Alfred Binet, as mental age divided by physical age (intelligence quotient), implies that developmental parameters, intimately entwined with traumatic learning, are of importance. Right from the beginning, intelligence-measuring instruments such as Binet's intelligence test and quotient, however, appeared to favor not males, but females!

In fact, to make intelligence tests "fair" with regard to gender, Binet eventually had to remove items that strongly favored females and add items that favored males. In effect, he and his successors had to "bias" the tests in order to make them apply equally to males and females. What exactly does this mean? Is development as well as intellect based on sex? And how can it favor females when all the available information suggested that if there were a bias, it should be toward the male, not the female? Perhaps the answer would surface in a closer examination of physical and developmental information.

While there are no statistically relevant differences in absolute size or weight of age-matched male and female brains, males typically have slower rates of bone growth and a later puberty, and attain full maturity at a later age than females, potentially as much as two years later. Slower development in animals has proven to be a biological predictor of greater mental plasticity and, to some extent, learning potential—not good news for equality of thought! But then, few have ever held that male and female thoughts were exactly the same or even similar, and it is interesting that this popular conclusion has been arrived at in society after society over time.

There are, however, some intriguing, clinically observable sex-based differences, and they include the following: Females have greater fine-motor coordination, and interestingly, fine-motor coordination tasks are often included in determinations of intelligence and memory. Female perception is biased toward people and faces, and male toward objects and designs. Females, at an earlier physical age, have a more highly developed auditory system, though there appear to be few differences in the visual system or its development. As a result, females seem to preferentially favor auditory, and males, visual object-data. Males' tendency to favor the visual/spatial over the auditory-linguistic mode would be expected to interfere with learning to read, a distinct challenge for many "normal" males, and later with learning to write, a skill that utilizes both reading and fine-motor coordination skills.

More specifically, female preference seems to be for language-based, explanatory learning, while males seem to prefer object-based, exploratory learning. The tendency of females to favor language-based, explanatory learning over object-based, exploratory learning would be expected to interfere with the development of nonlinguistic symbolic abstraction, which is critical for manipulating higher mathematics, a distinct challenge for many "normal" females; basic numeracy skills like counting and adding, however, should not be as affected, which in fact appears to be true.

These differences are repeatable and demonstrable. Interestingly, they are, in a sense, differences in *cognitive* styles. And even more interesting, they begin to result in measurable differences at about seven years of age, becoming most apparent at about eleven years of age—a time in adolescence when the effects of male and female hormonal systems are beginning to be fully reexpressed. On the other hand, the major difference between male and female cognitive styles after age eleven is that females rely on more reflectively acquired, ideational, auditory-based language pathways for acquiring knowledge. Girls are busy from an earlier age, at learning through talk. Males rely more on actively acquired, visual-tactile-based object-imaging pathways, and they are more busy physically exploring their environment firsthand.

At this same time, while society was struggling mightily with the idea that gender differences were forced by males onto females, and that the solution to fixing these apparent differences was legal and political, educators in all major disciplines, including the sciences and especially within the American public education system, were being influenced by John Dewey's mental investigations into bending education to fit industrial and postindustrial societies' needs.

Among clinicians, many were beginning to suggest that male and female brains must begin with a similar "floor plan" but somehow develop or organize their respective neural networks differently. To some physicians, including myself, while these differences were both affecting and being affected by metacognition, they were rooted in the nervous system and biological in nature—they had to be neurobiological. If true, this would have incredibly important implications for intelligence, traumatic learning, and ultimately all forms of effective learning. What was needed was not more ideas, but finding out what our own bodies were telling us. The problem was how to listen to what our brains were saying.

Chapter Five

What Our Bodies Tell Us

Up to this point, our focus has been on effective learning—traumatic, non-volitional, violational—and encompassing clinical evidence. From the first, we've steered clear of the veritable forest of educational ideations built on ideas and fantasies, and we've stayed focused on the physical—neurosensory-based observations about "real," effective learning as it actually occurs in individuals. In doing so, our perspective has been restricted to learning largely as clinicians see it: in people with exceptionally effective learning experiences. Now it's time to lift the curtain a bit on the raw stuff—the nitty-gritty of learning—the physical parts and pieces that make up the neurosensory learning system itself.

At this stage, experimental evidence is of particular importance. It helps us, once again, to gain a broader understanding of how and what we learn—what we are—by looking at exceptional situations under an experimenter's control. Unfortunately, along with exploring the experimental evidence comes the chance of burying our curiosity under mountains of contemporary data and information. So, in this chapter and the next, I will attempt to share with you what I have learned during my medical training and years of clinical practice about how the brain works.

A GREAT BIG PIECE OF OUR MIND

The studies we're going to discuss in this chapter were selected by me because (1) I've seen them at work in my practice; (2) I believe they shed significant light on effective learning—traumatic, therapeutic, and non-traumatic; and (3) they each uncover some new piece of the anatomy and neurobiology of learning. Please bear with me—I hope you will, you've come this far—and discover how traumatic learning can lead us to an entirely new, highly effective kind of nontraumatic learning. It is my hope that in doing so, you will acquire a basic vocabulary and appreciation for what actually happens above the eyes and between the ears when one learns. We can then spend the remainder of this chapter and the next applying it to effective learning in general, and to neurobiological learning in particular. Let's begin this next leg of our journey of discovery with two unusual, "natural" learning experiments: Victor and Genie.

Victor was discovered in the late 1800s in a forest. The facts of the case come to us through the eyes of Jean-Marc Itard, Victor's physician. When found, Victor was a "wild child": human in form, but naked of clothing and feral in behavior—in Itard's words, a raging, spitting, snarling, twelve-year-old mute savage. Victor's food preferences, lack of speech, and extensive scars strongly suggested that he had been in the wild for most of his life. It was assumed by everyone who saw him that he had been profoundly retarded since birth, and had therefore been abandoned. Incredibly, after years of intense work Victor began to respond intimately with other humans; in fact, he began to respond to learning methods used to teach the deaf. Victor eventually learned to speak simple words and even to read, but he never learned how to talk—at least as we think of it—in easy, meaningful sentences. Victor died in his forties, but the fascination surrounding him lasted into our century, where in 1980 Victor's life formed the basis of Francis Truffaut's movie *The Wild Child*. Incredibly, within two weeks of the movie's opening in Los Angeles, *another* twelve-year-old, mute "wild child" was rescued, this time not from a dark, savage forest, but from the asphalt jungle.

Tied to a "potty" chair for most of her life, "Genie" (as she was later dubbed) was rescued from ten years of solitary confinement in the back bedroom of a Los Angeles house. She had been beaten for making any noises. She sniffed, clawed, and constantly spat at her intended helpers. Genie had learned about objects by feeling them with her lips, as if she were blind. She seemed, for all intents, disconnected from her own human bodily sensations. Over time, and with considerable professional assistance, Genie eventually developed a way to communicate with others using vague labels. Like Victor, she never acquired a basic fluency in speech.

In both of these cases, we have demonstrated the power of "natural" and human-induced traumatic learning. While we stand at the dawn of actually understanding the functioning of the brain, we do not yet completely know the process of how these functions develop. In a sense, we are still wearing dark glasses in an educational Dark Age. We are blessed with more and more new data, and with an increasing number of competing theories to explain how human learning works—how it is that we are more than wild beasts. Victor and Genie suggest to me that while we may be close to understanding how the brain works, we are, by virtue of our traumatic learning experiences, little above other creatures with regard to awareness and the ability to discover and apply some form of effective *nontraumatic* learning to escape our otherwise fated lot.

I have had the wonderful opportunity of doing many things in my life—medicine, psychology, education, and linguistics. First and foremost I will always be a physician, bound by the Hippocratic Oath I swore when I graduated from medical school. Nowadays there are several such oaths, but when I graduated, we simply swore the Hippocratic Oath, said to be created by Hippocrates, the father of medicine, himself. Hippocrates developed many of his views on medicine from observing war, war trauma, and traumatic learning. We swore, first and foremost, to do no harm.

I believe that there can be no better mandate for redressing traumatic, violational learning and teaching than to take off our dark glasses and then, by our own volition, to walk from the darkness of traumatic learning into the light of a new kind of learning. Like Victor, Genie, and countless other survivors of trauma, the time has come—or rather is thrust on us. After all, who in their right mind would embark on such a journey *entirely* of their own accord? My extensive academic, medical, psychological, educational, and linguistic training hadn't adequately prepared me to understand the true extent of the vast power of traumatic learning and the extensive harm it causes. I have, however, come to grips with and begun to appreciate it over time, largely through the assistance of the courageous survivors of traumatic learning—especially the ones I have had the honor of working with, people not unlike Victor and Genie in terms of the perceived challenge before them. Salutations now aside, and with our eyes wide open, let's continue by looking at what was known about the human brain circa 1870.

Prior to 1870, it was known that the brain was composed of layers within layers. For millennia, the brain was considered to be like an onion, with its outermost layer being heavily convoluted, that is, folded, creating a vast surface—a huge tablet onto which one might write and record things. It was noted that humans had faster-growing and ultimately larger brains for their body size, compared with other animals (interestingly, this widely accepted view, when subject to more rigorous examination, has not proven entirely true). In fact, as we now know, humans, other primates, cetaceans, and elephants do not grow their brains faster than other animals; *they grow their bodies slower*. This has enormous implications for learning and for our clinical theory of developmental stages, phases, or levels of learning.

THE ORGANIZED BRAIN REORGANIZED

In the 1860s, scientists began to stimulate sections of the top surface of the human brain, the cerebral cortex (cerebrum—large brain; cortex—outside layer). This led to the successful separation and mapping of the gross-motor (conscious, whole-muscle action) and sensation strips, extending roughly from ear to ear along the top. It was quickly noted that selective destruction (in medical terms, ablation) of any portion of the motor strip, either naturally or experimentally, caused a flaccid or limp paralysis of some corresponding body muscles, whereas ablation of a corresponding area directly in front of the action strip caused spastic or tense paralysis and significantly degraded adjacent motor acts. This was a great "A-ha!" moment, confirming that areas of the human brain, indeed, had discrete functions.

Soon another strip was located, immediately adjacent to but just behind the gross-motor action strip: the sensory strip. The sensory strip was most unusual in terms of response to ablation. Sensory areas, when ablated, still allowed sensation, but mainly of raw neurologic data; for example, meaningless patterns of light, a voice heard as an unintelligible pattern of tones, or the touch of an object that failed to disclose to the mind any meaningful physical characteristics. These symptoms of stunted learning are eerily similar to Genie's concept of life with an unusual kind of touch. The results of this work are that an area key to the five classical senses—smell, sight, hearing, taste, and touch—was located. Even more interesting, the sensory strip turned out to roughly parallel the motor strip, immediately in front of it, and the premotor strip, immediately in front of the motor strip. I say "paralleled" in the sense that, for example, the premotor, motor, and sensory aspects of the mouth were located roughly on a horizontal line extending front to back across these three strips. Roughly, but not perfectly: not perfectly in terms of an exact location along the horizontal line or vertical strip, and not perfectly from person to person.

Continuing toward the back of the brain and corresponding head, the next strip, adjacent to and behind the sensory strip, are larger sensory *association* areas. These areas take up much of the lower sides and back portion of the brain, just in front of the backmost area, which records and stores visual object-data and associations. In general, the sensory association strip forges sensory data into object-images and to some extent symbols, complete with associations and meaning—for example, recognizing a particular person out of a crowd. This is the lodestone for what we've observed clinically: an area of stored—learned—memories, replete with object-data, associations, symbolism, and to some extent at least, interpretations and meanings—an area of true eidetic and interpreted memory.

A similar but more extensive and, we assume, more primitive or earlier developmental area is related to hearing object-data, associations, symbolism, and interpretation. This is the area that would be involved in Grandma's spoken advice, such as why God gave you two ears and only one mouth. It looks like it is located beneath but is also curved forward from the visual area. If you can imagine the cerebral cortex of the brain as a large, fat "C" with the eyes located in front of and facing outward from the open part of the C, then this hearing area would roughly correspond to the curved, bottom portion of the C. It is located inside the temples (sides) of the head and is referred to as the temporal area.

FROM BEYOND THE GRAVE

The front area of the brain (located in front of the gross-motor action strip) is appropriately called the *frontal association* or just *frontal* area. The frontal area provides combined and more complex integration than that of the sensory association area. We have learned much about this area from damage incurred by a historically common venereal disease: syphilis. A violent criminal, Al Capone, suffered from late-stage syphilis, which was destroying portions of his frontal areas. Syphilis also causes partial paralyses and disorders of mental clarity and induces a diminished sense of responsibility in personal affairs, slovenliness in personal habits, vulgarity in speech, and clownish behavior.

Historically nicknamed the "paresis of the insane," it unfortunately didn't interfere with Capone's ruthless intelligence. Ablation of the frontal areas or, more radically, destruction of the nervous fibers between the frontal areas and the interior of the brain has been demonstrated to change persistent anxiety into dull complacency, though at the cost of increased distractibility, decreased initiative, poor judgment, and lowered ethical standards. The frontal area should be beginning to sound a lot like an area of metacognition. And so it is!

With more discrete observations of injured and diseased brains, scientists discovered that *both* frontal and sensory association areas are vital to integrated, higher-level thinking and behavioral functioning. These two areas are particularly important in that they receive and transmit information to other areas of the brain. Collectively, nerve signals to any or all of these areas of the cerebral cortex (the outside of the large brain) are connected to the body by way of two major nerve "superhighways," which cross over right to left and left to right after passing back and forth through a sensori-emotional "gateway" called the thalamus (Greek: chamber), located deep inside the brain.

Physicians have grouped seemingly diverse sets of symptoms (things that patients talk about) and signs (things that physicians can see for themselves) into a Thalamic Syndrome. The condition is one in which there seems to be an oversensitivity to pain as well as the feeling of pain or discomfort associated with sensory, "gut" feeling, emotional or rhythmic stimuli, or even the absence of stimulation. Great shades of traumatic learning! This should be beginning to sound a lot like an area important to traumatic—violational—learning and teaching! And so it is!

So far our inner voyage has taken us roughly through the larger, upper brain, especially the outside layer (*cerebral cortex*), where much of what we experience as our conscious, willed existence is located, and deep into the middle of the large brain, where the *nerve superhighways* connect everything through the *thalamic gateway*.

There are, however, several other areas of the overall nervous system that impact almost equally on effective learning: the *cerebellum* (Latin: small brain; worm); the *"lower" brain stem* (the thalamus and attendant structures are sometimes considered part of the brain stem), where automatic (unconscious) control of the vital functions like breathing and awakening occur; and the *sympathetic nervous system*, a fourth "brain" consisting of a long line of very small, interconnected "brains" (medical: ganglia) located in the chest and abdomen, traveling along either side of the spine. But for the moment, let us continue exploring the cerebral cortex (the upper or larger brain), cerebellum, neural superhighways, and thalamus.

There are surprises from seeing the brain operate in such intricate, coordinated depths of control and referral. It's a twist on the old expression "The left hand doesn't know what the right hand is doing." The brain is especially prestidigitous: It's as if it has many arms and hands—a human octopus. There is more here to explore, but I would rather focus for a moment on some particularly interesting, almost uniquely human characteristics that result from this intricate coordination: speech and language.

Meta-analyses of ablative studies suggest evidence for a speech area, but not an "absolute" language area. Speech and language, bedrocks to our modern definitions of functional intelligence and learning, are not confined to the cerebral cortex. They often use and sometimes even require all of the "brain's" interconnected functioning. This complicates most teachers' simple view of learning and refutes the simplistic saying of GIGO ("garbage in, garbage out"), a computerized idea of human learning. So what does the brain have to say for itself?

TAKING SIDES

Well before the mid-nineteenth century, clinicians had noted the existence of two special "language" disorders, both involving a difficulty in remembering: One, called expressive aphasia (Greek: no speaking), involved difficulty in remembering how words are produced; the other, called auditory aphasia (not hearing speech), involved difficulty in remembering how words sound.

Around 1862, the physician and neurobiologist Paul Broca demonstrated that damage to a specific area of the front area of the cerebral cortex (near the bottom and just in front of the facial association strip) consistently elicited expressive aphasia. Oddly, damage to this area *on the left side of the brain* almost always caused the condition, while damage to the same area on the right side rarely did. People with damage to this specific area can find the words they want (they are stored elsewhere in the cerebral cortex), but are unable to understand or make a grammatically complex sentence. Speech consists almost entirely of content words. Broca gave us some understanding, but left us with a particularly perplexing puzzle—how to explain that *one-sided*, usually left, hemispheric damage caused expressive aphasia. At least Broca got his name attached to a very particular area of the brain, as other explorers got their names attached to mountains they were the first to climb. Maybe it's an apt analogy—we often talk of making "mountains out of molehills," and over time we have come to realize that Broca's area is, indeed, key to learning.

Less than a decade after Broca, another eminent physician and neurobiologist, Carl Wernicke, demonstrated the effects of damage to the temporal area, just inside the fold that makes the cerebral cortex into a "C." This time, damage causes auditory aphasia (loss of the ability to understand heard speech), but again, almost exclusively *on only the left side of the brain*.

It was also noted that clinically, after stroke damage to Broca's or Wernicke's area, the resulting aphasia didn't always last forever, and patients who recovered some, most, or all function didn't seem to have to go through all the classical developmental stages of language acquisition, like cooing, babbling, etc.

These observations resulted in the general agreement, *at that time*, on three fundamental "rules" of neuroanatomical brain function: Some specific areas seem associated with specific memories or behaviors. While the left and right sides appear to have grossly the same topography and internal anatomy, for some functions the left side seems to dominate the right. Finally, and most surprisingly, the return of lost language skills does not usually require one to go back through the "normal" development phases. This latter observation is most significant: It suggests that developmental phases and possibly learning steps, phases, or levels (and thereby learning itself) change with age.

Interestingly, none of these three ideas has proven entirely correct. More specifically, none entirely reflect the actual neurobiological processes involved. Yet my work as a clinician and educator in language acquisition tells me that these three ideas are fundamental to how teachers teach. I want to continue with these points in a moment. I want to emphasize that the limited truth of these points is also important. Once again, the physical evidence generally supports Werner, van der Kolk, Piaget, Montessori, and McGuinness, as well as our own clinical observations regarding traumatic or effective learning.

THE IMPORTANCE OF BEING EARNEST

The careful observation and study of aphasics and subsequent language acquisition was continued, this time by Eric and Elizabeth Lenneberg. The Lennebergs are famous developmental neurobiologists, whose contributions in two multicontributor, edited books entitled the *Foundations of Language Development* and *New Directions in the Study of Language* yielded several important treatment observations that, to this day, remain intriguing facts.

First, if aphasia strikes before about four years of age and the causative lesion is arrested, the learner often returns to a pre-language state and then proceeds back through all or most of the usual developmental stages of language acquisition, such as cooing, babbling, and naming, until speech is achieved.

Second, if it strikes and is arrested between roughly four and ten years of age, the learner can be expected to gradually recover speech over several years without going through the above developmental stages, *but only up to puberty*.

Finally, after puberty, new aphasiacs recover more quickly, often in a matter of months or, in the case of a prepubertal aphasia that has not yet cleared up completely, will basically stop further recovery, and any residual effects will become persistent.

After considerable searching (one might say brain scratching), two other specific areas of the brain were located that, if damaged, result in a loss of ability to comprehend the meaning of printed or written words, making reading and writing impossible. These discoveries suggested *at the time* that continued exploration would reveal specific sites for grammar, syntax, lexis, and phonology, and that other traditional aspects of language acquisition would eventually be located in the cerebral cortex. Sadly, this was yet another idea that, over time, would not prove entirely correct. It might as well have been on the surface of the moon. The brain began to not only elude, but positively delude researchers for a time—until, that is, the dawn of neuroelectrical instrumentation.

In the mid-twentieth century, neurosurgeon Wilder Penfield applied low-level electric current (Penfield's "lightning") to select areas of fully conscious, surgically exposed brains of epileptics, and thus created the first cerebral maps of language function. Using this technique, Penfield was also able to elicit—semi-consistently—body-memories and flashbacks in eight percent of his patients. The key is "semi-consistently."

In fact, while the specific points on any one individual's cerebral cortical map seemed consistent, when one person's map was compared to another's, there was more diversity than commonality. Penfield's lightning, applied to the same topographic area in different individuals, wasn't striking in the same place!

What was known in Penfield's time? First, there was no shortage of exceptional phenomena. About ten percent of persons demonstrated transient *or no language loss at all* after Broca's area damage (these were therefore assumed to have an aberrant Broca's area on the right side). Speakers of heavily inflected languages appeared less impaired by Broca's area damage (these were therefore assumed to have an aberrant cerebellum, contributing memories of the rhythmic component of inflection). And as a linguist myself, I could imagine the difficulties produced at that time by this discovery: Bilingual speakers with subsequent Broca's aphasia were impaired more in their native than their secondary language!

What was becoming clearer may seem intuitively obvious to the reader today: Learning is not organized strictly according to either brain architecture or linguistics. Some other form of neurofunctional organization has to be at play. If you've ever watched the detective show *Columbo*, you might guess how I was beginning to feel. It was getting harder and harder to leave any new suspect without saying, "Oh, I almost forgot to ask . . ." While the answer kept eluding me, I was always finding out *just one more thing.* By this point in my research, I had nearly completed my doctoral work in education in linguistics. My dissertation was outlined. But my brain seemed to have a voice of its own, demanding that I explain its workings in terms of how it actually works, not in terms of cool or fashionable ideas. I was challenging myself to step beyond the limits of imagination and back into the world of biophysical reality. To "see" the learning mind in its entirety, I had to go beyond mental ideations—beyond teaching. If it weren't for contemporary progress in brain imaging, I might never have been able to make that leap and invite you now to do the same with me.

THE WISDOM OF INNOCENCE

Despite wanting to "monkey around," humans differ from primates in several profound ways. First, our bodies and brains continue to grow long after birth. In spite of all we know about the evolution of a species (notice I say evolution *of a species*, not evolution *of species* in general), we have yet to predict when chimpanzees will begin to buy houses and commute to work. Maybe they are, in fact, surpassing us even as I write this, simply by refusing to buy houses and commute! We can, however, come to some conclusions about the human brain, its myriad elements, and its necessarily human favoritism. The neuro-organizational result of this favoritism appears to be a peculiar left-sided preponderance of both sensory and motor association areas.

Generally speaking, the *left* side of the body is represented in the *right* cerebral cortex, and *vice versa*. Neural fibers therefore crisscross from one side to the other as they approach and exit the brain. While damage to the one side of the brain often results in opposite-sided deficits, some things, speech and hearing, for example, are managed from one side in most persons—the "dominant" left side (remember that most people are right-handed). Clinical evidence, however, suggests that the brain, when damaged, will do whatever it can to reintegrate, even if that means changing hemispheric storage or function. There are many amazing stories about so-called "split brain" cases where, after specific left-brain area ablations, the brain has tried mightily to "right" itself but cannot.

Given the historical, experimental data presented thus far, you may at this point be encountering some counterintuition anxiety. Let's see now: One side of the brain, usually the left side, somehow establishes dominance over the other, but not always completely and with an option to change. Is that right? Yet this fits with clinical, experimental observations that removal of the entire left hemisphere of the brain in children, if done in early childhood, does not preclude near-normal language development, while the same in adults is usually, but not always, devastating. This presents a new and intriguing question: If the human brain is predispositionally left-sided, what are the associative areas of the right brain used for?

Removal of an entire right hemisphere demonstrated that (1) a few individuals suffered limited damage to language function; (2) about ten percent suffered extensive damage; and (3) roughly ninety percent developed problems with rapid visual pattern analysis, logic, contextualizing (e.g., getting jokes), rhythm, pitch, and emotional language.

The experimental evidence describes a situation where, in most people, one hemisphere, usually the left, establishes a generalized associative dominance very early in life, with regard to receptive and productive details of language. This dominance allows the other side, usually the right, to develop other "higher" elements, steps, phases, or levels of receptive and productive language. This situation is not, however, static. The right hemisphere anatomically and functionally maximizes between the age of two to about thirteen. Brain scans show that while the "average" male brain appears to follow this general pattern of specialization, the "average" female brain continues to utilize both hemispheres more diversely, and with increased regard to processing emotive language. Thus is born those puzzling, male "chick-flick" dating choices.

BRAIN GAMES: TAKING OUT THE TRASH

Applying the clinical and neuroanatomical information we have been developing to teaching would be a herculean task. Few teachers have any training in what you are reading about. It's therefore appropriate to ask, "Is it worth it, this upsetting of the educational apple cart?" If, in fact, the learning model we are developing is at all correct, then I think I can show you the proof—with the help of a little *more* information. Not just neuroanatomical (yes, neuroanatomical information is necessary), but some even more fundamental information about how brains, nervous systems, and bodies come together to actually accomplish learning.

Consider the experimental evidence from "agrammatism" (translation: "no word meaning"). Agrammatism is often associated with damage from stroke. Patients usually display mild to severe trouble with word choice, meaning, and ordering clues (technically, the latter should be called astructuralism). Specific brain damage, when it happens, is not commonly total. In fact, on careful clinical examination, grammar information does not actually appear to be "lost" or damaged at all, just less accessible.

Be that as it may, if grammar is stored in grammatical bytes, it is reasonable to ask where the lost "grammar" was before the stroke, and where it went afterward. New evidence suggests that the brain accommodates to speech by, for example, processing what some describe as "rates of changes," rather than individual bytes, objects, items, or data (like phonemes). Loss of an associative brain region should result in loss of a specific sensation, word, thought, grammatical rule, behavior, or function. But no: Whatever remains intact within a damaged area appears to be suddenly free for subsequent use, and what's of paramount importance is that these newly freed areas *are* used!

Truly deaf individuals, for instance, can deliberately develop (using cognitive learning, for a start) *left-sided auditory* associative areas to enhance visual, tactile, taste, or olfactory functions. Individuals who have lost *both* sight and hearing have left-sided visual and auditory associative areas freed up to acquire enhanced tactile (e.g., signing), taste, or olfactory function. If people with physical disabilities can benefit from rigorously directed learning that targets specific areas of the brain, then what benefits would occur for people who do not have disabilities?

In a practical sense, what teachers often seem to strive for, the "Holy Grail" of teaching, is a means of focusing the information like a laser beam and burning it into the brain, irrespective of how and where the brain would "naturally" locate it. If we think of the brain as an individual puzzle, the pieces of which are located in the natural world, teaching as we know it today makes little sense. Students desperately need to become better at recognizing the different "shapes" inherent in each individual's brain puzzle. Teaching and traumatic learning effectively override everything, but the side effects, once recognized, are simply too damaging. While individual human brains are amazingly similar with regard to structure (anatomy) and the way they process what they sense, they are quite different, even unique, in terms of what they learn from a particular learning event—like the three blindfolded men who were told to identify an elephant hidden behind a screen. The first felt its trunk and said it was snakelike. The second felt its foot and said it was treelike. The third, its ear . . . This is beginning to approach the inevitable "nature versus nurture" question, isn't it? OK, then, another question: Do exceptionally intelligent people have bigger brains, or do they just better use what we all have? Where does one start? Think "Rain Man"—think "*idiot savant*."

Experimental evidence fails to reveal any new structures or "extrasized" areas in idiot savants. In fact, aside from natural, acquired, or "old age" damage, no statistically significant differences in gross anatomic structures have been consistently found. Destruction of one area appears to provide "free space" for other areas to grow into. Impairment of one learning "strategy" appears to provide extra resource space for development of another complementary, or even mutually-exclusive, learning strategy—a sort of Machiavellian zero-sum neurobiological strategy.

Postmortem studies on geniuses such as Albert Einstein have similarly failed to show consistent, significant differences in size, weight, or gross anatomic features (there have been differences below this level, but most people have differences at these lower anatomic levels, too). These findings are not, of course, conclusive—after all, a genius could someday show up with a very different-looking brain—and then, of course, I would have to consider changing this statement. But for now, the bulk of evidence weighs against "nature."

Lateralization, on the other hand, may well be more an adaptation of the brain *to* language than an adaptation of the brain *for* language (this idea will be revisited again later, as it directly impacts two widely acknowledged contemporary theories of learning: Chomsky's Universal Grammar Theory and Gardner's Theory of Multiple Intelligences). Through language, we all share the seeds of genius.

BEGINNING BACK AT THE BEGINNING

It is generally accepted that "ontogeny recapitulates phylogeny." That is, all living beings pass through stages of evolution during their early development. If true, then there should be some leftover embryonic footprints of the neurobiological architecture that underlies effective learning. We will use a new understanding of the neurodevelopmental and embryological origins of the human nervous system to expand later on the clinical and experimental evidence. But before we do, as the Cheshire Cat suggested to Alice lost in Wonderland, one should begin at the beginning.

Humans begin as a *totipotent*, single-celled organism that quickly grows into a ball, which forms a furrow (technically, invaginates) to form the future nervous system. Based on animal and mammalian studies, under the influence of as few as five genes, the "head" end of the nervous system rapidly differentiates. As it develops further, the embryonic nervous system forms a short, smooth tube called the "brain stem," followed by a longer future spinal cord.

These embryonic areas eventually shape into (1) a cerebrum—two large brain hemispheres constituting the conscious or "main brain"; (2) a cerebellum—two smaller brain hemispheres located below and behind the cerebrum that constitute the "rhythmic brain"; (3) the thalamus, which along with some specialized substructures called the hypothalamus, hippocampus, cingulate gyrus, and amygdala, makes up a learning "gateway"; (4) a left and right major nerve "superhighway"; (5) the brain stem; and (6) the "sympathetic" nervous system. Within the first two are two exceptional embryonic developments: a *conscious*, pyramidal system (so named because the major cerebral brain cells often appeared pyramid-shaped) and an *unconscious*, extrapyramidal system, which maintains automated and semi-automatic bodily functions such as regular breathing, storing, filtering, checking, recognizing, and maintaining rhythmic neuron-firing patterns.

Many sensations (a finger pinprick, for example) travel to the cerebrum via the nervous superhighway. On the way, they cross over to the other side and pass through the thalamic learning gateway and on to the brain. Some neurosensory impulses are directed first to the cerebellum, and then either back down the brain stem and spinal cord to the body, or up to the cerebrum, again via the nervous superhighway by way of the thalamic gateway.

The cerebral cortex—the outer layer of the cerebrum—contains two "maps" of the human body, one for sensations, and just in front of it, one for muscles. The "muscle map" is actually the "driver's seat" of conscious muscular activity. Nerve fibers travel to the neurosensory, and from these neuromuscular mapping areas and the body via the major nerve superhighways. All pass through the thalamic learning gateway.

OK, so at this point, if you are feeling a little overwhelmed, rest assured, you're not the first or only one! Actually, in the late 1970s an attempt was made to simplify this neurosensory-muscular maze, resulting in a popular theory called the Triune Brain.

The Triune Brain Theory *is* simple and handy, as well as easy to teach, explain, and use. Unfortunately, much of what we've discovered clinically and experimentally about how neurobiological learning actually occurs within the human brain no longer fits this theory very well. Still, I would like to take a moment and describe the theory anyway, not just because of its past popularity, but because it is actually a good jumping-off place.

The Triune Brain is based on a tripartite division of the central nervous system into a "human" (cerebral, neo-cortical, or neo-mammalian) brain, a "mammalian" (paleo-cortical, limbic [thalamic—hypothalamic— amygdalic], or paleo-mammalian) brain, and a "reptilian" (brain stem) brain. Catchy, but the idea that we are basically reptiles with regard to behavior, or that there are "reptilian" urges alive within us, doesn't cut it. I have also heard it said that we are basically birds (after all, birds are assumed to have evolved from reptiles) in our behaviors, and that somewhere inside each of us lives a "birdbrain." I rather suspect the bird argument is merely the swan song of the Triune Brain Theory. Jokes aside, if the Triune Brain Theory has excited your curiosity or interest, then I believe it's done pretty much what it was designed to do.

Let's look more at the Triune Brain approach. Simply put, the three parts of the brain are viewed as having developed from, and are thereby representative of, lowest (reptilian), middle (limbic or learning system), and highest (neo-mammalian) steps, phases, or levels of consciousness. That sounds somewhat familiar, at least!

The neo-mammalian brain (ideationally, the conscious thoughts and behaviors that make us "human") would have to include therefore our frontal, pre-sensory, sensorimotor, parietal, temporal, and visual cortices, along with all higher thoughts, associations, interpretations, and metacognitive knowledge and wisdom that account for our ability to empathize, plan, create, reason, judge, be compassionate, and love—everything we would traditionally look toward teachers (and daytime television) to provide.

The paleo-mammalian brain ("paleo" meaning ancient), or limbic system, would include everything that is necessary for our primary survival. This is where immunity and the fight-or-flight responses would rest, and where our primary learned reflexes would be learned and stored.

The brain stem, or reptilian brain, on the other hand, is all about the base urges—those base drives that makes us one animal among many. Sex, territoriality, and many of the traumatic stress responses fundamental to effective learning would reside here; the very basis for traumatic learning would be located in the reptilian brain.

When stated this way, the *idea* of a Triune Brain, like Freud's idea of the id, ego, and superego, despite its simplicity and rhetorical appeal, is grossly insufficient to explain what we already know about exceptional learning and how it must physically occur. Furthermore, it results in few really productive hypotheses and predictions, and no new learning principles or methodologies—unless you count the *National Enquirer* theory of reptilians among us.

If the brain is not a triune brain, then what is it? Based on clinical and experimental evidence (drumroll, please), it appears to me that the human brain is quite a few things other than triune. There are at least eight basic observations that must be accounted for.

First, the brain, and much of the rest of the human nervous system, is multipotential.

Second, it is multiply redundant.

Third, it consists of at least two quasi-integrated subsystems, one centered in the cerebral cortex, dealing with object-data, associations, symbols, and conscious thought, the other in the cerebellar cortex, dealing with rhythmic data and associations.

Fourth, there are major nerve fiber superhighways to, from, between, and within these and the brain stem subsystems, which appear to pass through a thalamic-hypothalamic-amygdalic gated portal that exerts some form of control over what is effectively learned.

Fifth, the system itself is embryogenically and developmentally rebuilt from a prototypic, general genetic plan.

Sixth, the emerging form becomes highly individualized according to resources available to each individual at very specific developmental stages.

Seventh, specific areas may be used and reused to store and process a single object-datum (rare), multiple object-data (also rare) and multiprocessed, associated, symbolic, interpreted information (intriguingly common).

Finally, the *entire* system is the result of millions of years of use under constant traumatic, evolutionary pressure, including birth trauma.

Triunism can't even begin to address most of these observations, and it can't directly answer perhaps the most fundamental question of all: How does a brain organize its more than a trillion cells in order to learn effectively? And, since I am posing this question in the context of what is known medically, clinically, anatomically, and experimentally, the answer will need to address each of these, as well as reflect the actual physical structure and workings of the brain. So I guess it's time for me to step up and state my own case. OK, here's what we know so far.

FIRMWARE AND HARDWIRING

The body's learning system is more than just a brain and nerves. To start with, let's roughly divide it into a fixed neuroelectrical system and a circulating neurochemical system.

The fixed neuroelectrical system is called, by most clinicians, the human nervous system. It is roughly divided into a central and a peripheral nervous system. The central nervous system includes everything neuroelectrical that is located in the central axis of the body, namely the brain and spinal cord.

The central nervous system begins with the brain. The brain is normally divided into the cerebrum (the "big," volitional brain—I have used the medical term here because it seems to have at last crept into general use) and the *rhythmic brain* (the "little" brain, or cerebellum).

The cerebrum is anatomically divided into an outside portion (technically, the cerebral cortex) and an inside portion consisting of the *nerve superhighways* (nerves), a *thalamic gateway* (an area that selects which electrical impulses should be stored and where to store them), and a *brain stem* (the center for the most important automatic activities, like breathing, and a conduit to the spinal cord). These areas are anatomically identifiable.

The cerebrum is also divided more *functionally* (but not necessarily anatomically) into various surface areas, which I shall call, starting from the forehead, bilateral *frontal* (interpretive and metacognitive) areas; followed by *parietal* (side) areas consisting of a motor strip (nerves initiating and carrying electrical impulses—commands—from the brain to the body), a sensory strip (nerves receiving and carrying electrical impulses—

sensations—from the body to the brain), and a general information storage area; a back or *occipital* area where object-data, associative, and interpretive visual information are stored; and finally, folded underneath on the sides and coursing back toward the front, the *temporal* areas, where object-data and associative and interpretive auditory information are processed and to some extent stored. I don't think this sounds much like a combination new, ancient, and reptilian brain, do you? It does, however, make surprising sense with regard to what we know about clinical traumatic learning.

In addition to these functional surface areas, the cerebrum is also divided, anatomically and functionally, from the outside to the inside into six layers.

The first layer (indicated anatomically by the Roman character for one—"I") is a narrow outside layer consisting of densely packed, heavily insulated nerve fibers. These fibers originate elsewhere within the brain or body; there are a few round neurons interspersed.

Layer II contains large numbers of small, densely packed, pyramid-shaped neurons.

Layers III through V contain fewer but still quite impressive numbers of *vertically ordered*, larger, longer, pyramid-shaped neurons, interconnecting within layers and also between layers.

Layer VI is a particularly deep layer, containing intermediate numbers of small, multiply oriented, multishaped neurons. Each layer can, and does, vary between individuals and, within any one individual, over time.

Now let's take a brief but closer, more critical look at these layers and their possible functions. Layers II and IV look like what might be expected of a brain storing data in a one-datum-one-neuron form. On the other hand, just based on the numbers, we would quickly run out of learning "space" and have to quit thinking. I know you're thinking right now, "I know someone just like this!" Yes, well . . .

Layer II neurons receive a number of long neural fibers from the major neural superhighways that pass through the thalamic system on their way to and from the cerebellum, brain stem, and body—a sort of interconnected input system. This doesn't sound at all like either a one-datum-one-neuron or tripartite brain; what it sounds like is a well-controlled neurosensory learning system. Similarly, Layer V neurons are the origin of a number of motor functions involving such distant muscles as the fingers and toes. Layer VI appears to be a primary interconnection area where fibers from all over the body, including peripheral sensory organs, internal body organs, brain stem, cerebellum, thalamus, and even primitive smell, come together, interdigitate, and then pass on throughout the brain. Finally, neurons within Layers III to IV clearly interdigitate both within their layer and between other layers. Taken together, this architecture appears to me to be organized in a form in line with my eight key observations—and that fits with clinical levels of metacognition in the frontal areas and with object-data, association, symbolism, and interpretation levels in others.

The cerebellum has not been as widely studied as the cerebrum, but it appears to be at least loosely organized in multiple, interconnected levels by types or patterns of rhythms.

The thalamic gateway—the thalamus and hypothalamus (located below the thalamus)—as well as a number of intimately associated anatomical areas such as the hippocampus and amygdala, are all clinically involved in the selection of what and how to remember. Interestingly, these areas ultimately activate the entire nervous system, and are activated by fight-or-flight "trauma" hormones produced under control of the sympathetic nervous system.

Collectively, the thalamic gateways seem capable of "upping the neuroelectrical ante" in an upward spiraling fashion, until a certain neuroelectrical energy level is reached, which results in effective learning in various areas of the brain. Among trauma psychologists, it is often held that the thalamus-hypothalamus-hippocampus-amygdala axis is directly involved in traumatic learning, specifically in terms of learned data and information, and in the learning process.

There you have it: a neuroanatomical synopsis of the central nervous system (CNS). But wait, there's more. It's now time to examine what we know neuroanatomically of the peripheral nervous system.

The peripheral nervous system (PNS) consists of all neurons and nerve fibers located outside the CNS. As such, it consists of (1) the spinal nerves, both sensory and motor, that are extensions of CNS neurons; (2) an autonomous or "autonomic" nervous system; and (3) the circulating neurochemical system (technically, the "hormone system").

Spinal nerves complete the neuroelectrical circuitry necessary for reflexes and reflex learning to occur. They act like peripheral wires, connecting the various parts of the body with the various parts of the nervous system. While a necessity, they are in and of themselves insufficient for the establishment, firing, and coordination of reflexes. Most clinicians today, for example, agree that a thalamic gateway or axis is also required in order to establish and express a coordinated reflex.

In addition to the spinal nerves, a largely externalized *autonomic nervous system* exists, complete with two diffusely distributed "brains." A chain of small brains (ganglia) called the sympathetic nervous system is located on either side of the spinal column. Numerous individual ganglia, collectively referred to as the parasympathetic nervous system, are located more peripherally, close to the muscles they control. These two systems, in a general sense, functionally oppose each other.

Anatomically, the *sympathetic nervous system* enervates organs involved in fighting or fleeing. For example, sympathetic nerves dilate (enlarge) the pupils, speed up the heart rate, dilate the airways, and stimulate the adrenal medulla, located just above the kidneys, to produce epinephrine (adrenaline—of "adrenaline rush" fame) and other fight-or-flight hormones.

These *circulating neurochemicals* quickly spread throughout the body, preparing it for fight or flight and at the same time lowering the thalamic gateway's threshold for triggering reflex behavior and the initiation of effective (in this case, traumatic) learning. Notice how these systems work together to maximize the fight-or-flight reflexes and traumatic learning. This may sound animalistic, but it's quite sophisticated and hardly reptilian.

While my earlier eight observations may only be "scratching the surface" of learning, they seem to fit these real, physical structures much better than a triune brain. Beyond just a lot of criticism of other theories of teaching, we are in fact beginning to establish a reality-based, neurobiological foundation for effective learning.

CRITICAL TIMES, CRITICAL PERIODS

You've now studied a millennium or more of information about how the brain develops, its basic physical design, and how that design fits what we have observed clinically about traumatic learning. The challenge now is to apply these collectively to the stages, phases, or levels of learning *as they actually occur during effective learning.*

Learning appears to occur differently in infants than in children, and between females and males, especially during and after puberty. We must now examine and, if real, account for these differences. The human body goes through a staggering amount of developmental change from a fetus to a mature adult, which should be reflected in distinctive differences in learning and education. These differences, if relevant, should be reflected in observable physical changes at the organ, tissue, cellular, biochemical, and/or electrical level. They should also appear in "normal" as well as traumatized learners, in traumatic as well as nontraumatic situations, and during traumatic as well as traditional institutional and nontraumatic learning, whether being learned traumatically or otherwise.

It is time to focus on effective learning in the undamaged, developing brain of early to late adolescent learners. What exactly must happen before puberty to make post-pubertal learning effective? How exactly is effective learning different after the onset of puberty than before it? For the answers to these and similar questions, we must turn to a new generation of experimental neurotechnology: that of biological and medical-imaging studies.

Chapter Six

What Machines Are Saying about Us

Brain-imaging technology, and the ability to observe the brain *working*, is, in its own way, akin to giving clinicians and educators a Hubble telescope that can look into the body and see learning at its very beginning. I am personally blown away when I actually see a patient's brain create mental impulses, knowing that such impulses are at that very same instant occurring in my own mind. It's as close to shared omniscience as mere mortals will probably ever get. But even with this technology in its infancy, I can already envision many consequences undoubtedly far exceeding anything presently imaginable. Isaac Asimov always challenged us to consider what our lives will be like when we're living with androids—humanlike robots. But that's nothing, compared with being totally naked in thought before them.

The breakthroughs described in this chapter are new, but like so many modern marvels, they owe their existence to fundamental work from as far back as the 1920s. Let's jog through this brief historical period and then begin confidently exploring how imaging technology can further clarify what we know about effective learning.

CAPTURING THE MIND AT WORK

In 1924, the German physician-psychiatrist Hans Berger expanded on the Dutch physiologist Willem Einthoven's basic but very famous technique for recording generalized bioelectrical activity. Berger attempted to record human brain waves from the surface of the head. This was a profound advance, since no one really knew for sure exactly how brains worked. Much of the popular evidence of the day was pointing toward some kind of new form of "psychic" energy, called psi.

Berger's production of "simple" electrical maps of the brain was simply stunning! Not only did it appear that the brain used common electrical energy, just like lightbulbs, automobiles, and other invented machines, but by using mapping "coordinates," Berger actually documented different patterns of electrical activity in different parts of the brain at different times. This technology literally exploded, and a rash of neuroelectrical recording devices resulted: "lie detectors" based on galvanic skin response; "thought detectors" using event-related potential; "bio-energy brain scans" using magnetoencephalometers; even "thought therapies" like transcranial magnetic stimulation. Berger's work was more than food for thought; it was thought itself, caught in the act.

Brain imaging as we think of it today actually began in the 1930s with "NMR" (nuclear magnetic resonance), the brainchild of physicists Felix Bloch and Edward Purcell (they later shared a Nobel Prize for their discovery). NMR devices create a strong pulse of electromagnetic energy, which is absorbed and then released by subatomic nuclei as they return to their original state. These studies eventually paired with another, now widely accepted marvel of our age: cost-effective and accessible computer time. The result was the creation of sophisticated computers that could reassemble the NMR data into a stack of photographlike images, *et voilà*: Three dimensional images resulted that could be assembled into a moment-to-moment "video" of what was going on inside a brain!

In 1967 another marriage of convenience wedded the well-known, two-dimensional X ray that most of us have had taken at one time or another at the hospital once again with computers. This work, by a British electrical engineer, Sir Godfrey Hounsfield, resulted in the computed axial tomography (CAT) scanner—a device that could produce three-dimensional X rays of the body's interior, allowing doctors a way to directly view the organs of the internal body without surgery. Even more amazing, it became possible to rotate and examine a brain image from virtually any angle. CAT studies are responsible for some of my own "cat's-eye" views of the neuroanatomical learning processes in the last chapter.

In 1974, expanding on Bloch and Purcell's work, Raymond Damadian, one of Purcell's graduate students and a physician, devised a way to create a stronger and more uniform magnetic field followed by small pulses of electric current that would cause the spin of test material nuclei to *wobble* slightly. Again computers, now increasingly called "brainlike," were used to assemble the data into photographlike images. But it suddenly got better: To show how the brain actually caused the body to move, images were taken as someone performed a task. This neat trick was immediately dubbed *functional* magnetic resonance imaging (fMRI). Functional MRIs quickly grew to be so sensitive that they could measure minute changes in blood flow, tissue oxygen levels, even the structure of individual brain proteins. The resulting images were more than worth a thousand words: they were glimpses of the tiny neurochemical events that actually represented learned data and information. With the help of these machines, humans could begin to actually stare, face-to-face, at the smallest elements of raw learning *in its physical form*, and to "see" something so astounding that no one had ever before dared to imagine: human thoughts, knowledge, and wisdom.

Again beginning in the 1970s, another approach to brain imaging, called positron emission tomography (PET), surfaced, proving that we were in fact barking up the right tree. PET is an invasive technique, requiring injection of a radioactive sugar. Placed in an immense magnet called a cyclotron, individual tissues to small groups of cells could be spotted even *as they used the sugar to learn!* The advantage of PET studies is that the results, while less specific than with fMRI, are the direct result of brain activity.

Yet another different approach surfaced in the 1970s: For decades researchers, writers, and the public toyed with the idea of "psychic biomagnetism." The problem wasn't whether or not it existed. The problem was that magnetic changes that occurred within biological organisms were one hundred thousand to one hundred million times smaller than the earth's magnetic field within which we are surrounded. Massachusetts Institute of Technology researcher David Cohen is credited with finally recording the first magnetoencephalogram (MEG), using a hatlike device in a specially insulated room in conjunction with a huge magnet called a cyclotron and an fMRI. MEGs actually sense naturally occurring magnetic field changes caused by brain activity. Best of all, these images occur actively and are sensed in near real time (less than one millisecond). This allowed the "filming" of small group of cells as they process learning events. As of this moment, the newest development in MEG is the use

of low- and high-temperature superconducting quantum interference devices (SQUIDs). These are undoubtedly the most sensitive magnetic field
detectors ever developed. Eventually, these and next-generation devices
will let us observe the process of learning at the level of a single neuron!

Around 1985, Anthony Barker, Reza Jalinous, and Ian Freeston announced a way of electrically stimulating specific brain regions using a directed magnetic field located outside the head. Transcranial magnetic
stimulation (TMS) and repetitive TMS (rTMS) were quickly noted to
have some special advantages over all the other approaches thus far. First,
TMS can temporarily inactivate a specific brain area—which allows the
validation of PET, fMRI, and MEG data—an electronic "second opinion,"
so to speak. Second, TMS allows the exploration of reflex behavioral, as
well as sensory, kinesthetic, and cognitive pathways. Third, rTMS provides a way to explore the effects of timing and rhythm on neural activity.
Fourth, it requires less cooperation, and can therefore be used on children,
infants, newborns, even fetuses, and to explore learning in other animal
species. Finally, it has opened the door to new therapeutic approaches to
traumatic learning.

So where will we be ten years from now? The next generation of inductive neurosensory learning devices may well be some advancement of
noninvasive, near-infrared, multipoint spectroscopy (NIMPS) of the brain,
first reported by the German physician Arno Villringer in the early 1990s.
I suspect that our device of the future will be somewhat like an interactive
learning imagery and augmentation device (ILIAD)—just the thing for
thought surgeons to work on the most fundamental stages, phases, and
levels of learning.

All the technology in the world is no good, however, without better
techniques. Perhaps you will recall a commercial in which a master diamond cutter is seen sitting in the back seat of a luxury car. He had seen
and studied images of the diamond's facets, and like any diamond cutter
worth his salt, he knew exactly where the diamond needed to be cut. But
it took expert technique to do it in the back of a car rumbling through
Manhattan. Like the case of the diamond cutter, three particularly important imaging techniques have recently been developed. Taken together
with technology advances, they will almost certainly vastly expand the
experimental frontiers of learning research.

First, there are some new techniques based on a subject's (even a newborn's) directed visual attention, for example, measuring line of sight, du-

ration of viewing, switching speed, and viewing pattern. Using these techniques in conjunction with the latest in imaging technology, it is possible to correlate brain activity with cognitive interest and resultant learning. This particular technique is all the more intriguing in view of the almost universal "infantile amnesia," from an adult point of view, that prevents us from remembering in detail how learning occurs during the first three years of our lives.

Second, new techniques are emerging to control the presentation of sensory dissimilarities during learning. The widely held illusion that learning is based on recognition and establishment of similarities is, even as I write, being challenged. It appears more and more that learning is actually based on the constant scanning for (curiosity) and "catching" of (discovery) *dissimilarities.* This technique is in vigorous development. I have more than just a suspicion; I have my own clinical observations on traumatic learning, which strongly suggest that this will prove one of the keys to understanding and applying effective learning.

Third, there is the use of the newly emerging repetition suppression (RS) technique. RS fMRI studies have already begun isolating small columns of neurons, and even individual neurons, during learning. For example, specific neurons have been identified in the parietal (upper side) areas of the cerebrum that were used to store numeric object-data and number-symbols.

So here we are: reasonably knowledgeable about the newest brain-imaging technologies and even some of the newest techniques for their application. We're now fully prepared for the last leg of our journey back in time, and we will soon stand poised to make the leap from traumatic to effective nontraumatic learning. All that stands in our way is . . . us.

FROM THE MINDS OF BABES

Brain-imaging studies, in my opinion, leave no room to imagine learning as something occurring principally or even mostly in a classroom. Collectively, these studies have had a galvanizing effect on my own sense of what effective learning is, and ultimately should be.

The Western philosopher John Locke is credited with the famous metaphor that newborn minds are *tabulae rasae*, blank tablets, onto which knowledge is written. In director Lesley Ann Patten's film *Words of My*

Perfect Teacher, the teacher, an incarnate lama in the Tibetan Buddhist tradition named Dzongsar Khyentse Norbu (a representation of His Eminence Dzongsar Jamyang Khyentse Rinpoche), says that the mind is where suffering, closed hearts, and prejudice begin. Is everything we know obtained through suffering, and must it inevitably result in closed hearts, entrenched views, and prejudice?

According to Locke, newborns are like vast sponges, or blank computer disks, ready to absorb whatever's given them. A newborn's mind, these views say, has no recourse to a priori data, schemes, or frames of reference. We've explored much of the hardware, firmware, and hardwiring. Where does the "software" come from? How exactly do newborns make sense of the cataclysmic new world into which they find themselves so suddenly and traumatically plunged?

Perhaps they aren't really blank tablets. Newborns have at various times in history been considered primitive and even miniature adults. This belief regularly resurfaces in an egalitarian, legalistic society such as ours. Perhaps it is part of an innate, desperately driven search for equality in equality. All "necessary" knowledge, according to this line of thinking, is intuitively stored inside, waiting only for the "right" newborn, moment, or teacher to be fortuitously "unlocked"—an idea as old as time and as new as the linguistic theories of Noam Chomsky and Steven Pinker.

There's also the romantic idea that newborns, as evidenced by their cherubic nature, have access to a unique kind of knowledge: an openness, innocence, spirituality, or childishness, which makes them "special" learners, this age of specialness lasting only until a loss of innocence occurs.

Infants and children have also been considered by some philosophers, educators, and even their parents to be superintelligent learners who, in the course of learning about the world, lose a part of themselves and become human (except possibly to siblings who know them for who they really are).

Or, yet again, there is the idea that they are all fragile, limited, uniquely structured proto-learning systems, to which adults must learn to adjust and adapt in order to physically imprint ideas into their otherwise wasted, or even mindless, brain structure.

It has always surprised me that we are so inclined to want to, and in many cases actually, believe every new, fashionable idea, while at the same time spitefully ignoring or at best repressing the realities of our physical world revealed through our senses. For example, for centuries virtually all mainstream schools of psychology and education have rejected most of (or more accurately, have mostly ignored) the fact that babies learn prior to birth. Fewer yet bother with the idea of birth as a major trauma, let alone birth and subsequent trauma as deeply affecting every human's as well as humanity's accumulated learning.

I have tried my best to present physically based clinical and experimental evidence, not just ideas, that strongly suggests otherwise. But while I hope you are with me in regarding the physically based evidence as incredibly tantalizing, without something more solid it still lacks what many researchers call "hard substance." Then, lo and behold, along comes brain-imaging studies. With them the whole concept of prenatal, birth, and traumatic learning resurfaces, this time in what I hope you will agree with me is a more compellingly substantive form. But enough ideas! It's time to look at the specific contributions that contemporary experimental imaging studies have made to our understanding of effective learning and how they directly affect human knowledge.

I admit that the biological literature on prenatal learning is sparse — some would say still too sparse for definitive conclusions . . . and yet, this cuts both ways. Perhaps with what we now know, it's also too early to justify our dismissing it, like we are accustomed to doing. For example, there's Emma Werner's children of Kauai — some of the first "hard," statistical, clinically based field evidence that perinatal trauma results in effective learning. It didn't end there.

Physician-researcher Yolanda P. Graham and her colleagues, as well as medical researchers Leonie Welberg and Jonathan Seckl, have recently announced clinical *and* experimental evidence of perinatal thalamic gateway reprogramming.

And as for my own observations about neonatal pain mentioned earlier, they are being more fully described by physician-researcher-educators even as I write, right down to the neuroanatomical and biochemical pathways necessary to create repressed and/or cyclically resurfacing memories of that pain. What is clear to me is that something we can loosely call prenatal learning has been occurring since way back in our evolutionary history, and is still occurring today — every day! Even before we were born, imaging suggests, we were already precocious, communicating in every way we knew, with whomever we thought would listen.

Being born is hard on the mother, newborn, and even witnesses. Several long-term studies (and my observations agree with them) say that the birth event is not only a significant learning event, but perhaps *the* single most significant learning event in our entire lives. This one event establishes the whole process of effective traumatic learning and teaching within us. Thus begins the teaching-learning debate, like a card game—with one "winner" and everyone else "losers"—ultimately favoring the multibillion-dollar "business" of education. This process is not simply established; it continues to expand and to rage on.

For some reason absolutely baffling to me, within this debate there also remains a widespread bias toward viewing the birth event as "normally" traumatic. Normally traumatic? Now that's an oxymoron if I ever heard one! I don't think I want either "normal" or "abnormal" trauma, thank you very much! I would vastly prefer something, maybe anything, else. In spite of lingering societal, psychological, educational, and even medical arguments *against* the primal importance of birth trauma, I still regard the fact that most humans experience amnesia surrounding the birth event, often extending up to the first three years of life, as an indication of the intensity, extent, importance, and traumatic nature of this primary learning event.

IF I KNEW THEN WHAT I KNOW NOW . . .

Some Americans, decades ago, used to tease about the Japanese penchant for education of the *very* young. Now one can purchase an in vitro sound machine at a local Babies 4 U store in order to provide a developing fetus with classical music by which to develop (OK, there's really no such store, but it is possible to get such a device). Wouldn't you know it, "Bach's baby boom" (or should that be "Bach's baby bloom"?) owes much to the experimental data we're looking at in this chapter.

After recovering from the shock of the birth event (and whatever it means to each "normal" participant), newborns almost immediately begin visually focusing on faces (as well as on any facial-like patterns) presented within one foot of their face. Some researchers argue (unconvincingly in my mind) that babies are just "normally" neonatally nearsighted. While it is true, I think there is inarguably more to this behavior than just default looking. The literature seems to agree with my own years of experience as a pediatrician, that babies are actually imitating facial patterns and rely heavily on specific, peripheral, visual learning cues such as movement, timing, and rhythm. They actually show a *learning preference* for irregular "stop and go" presentations of a learning object, and they learn even better when accompanied by simultaneous sound- and touch-based neurosensory experiences. This implies steps, phases, or levels of learning.

Newborns have amazingly intact senses of both visual (sight) and auditory (hearing) perception: they actually know, like little tennis players, center versus periphery, foreground versus background. Newborns have an affinity—a *learning preference*—for new or unusual visual objects, sounds, and sensations. They quickly acquire sufficient visual/auditory acuity and discrimination to recognize their mother's face, the gaze of her eyes, and they *almost immediately begin imitating observed lip movement—smacking sounds*. It's true: kids do say the darnedest things. But what's really important is that we are discovering that they say it earlier than we ever imagined! Interestingly, the first human languages—"protolanguages"—seem to be based on smacking and clicking sounds. These observations have led many to conclude that newborn behavior is genetic. It might look like it, but genetics has not proven to be the source for all this inspiring baby talk.

Before beginning my clinical studies in effective, traumatic learning, I believed that genes surely played *the* substantive role in baby learning. I've since found out that there is little need to resort to "genetic behavior" to explain a newborn's ability to distinguish objects. For example, using another interesting brain-imaging approach called evoked response potential, or ERP, it's been shown that nine-week-old babies can learn to recognize new faces in a matter of minutes, distinguish basic vowel sounds, and become easily distracted, even excited, by unusual peripheral sensory objects. Infants at this age are not only learning rudimentary data and objects, they are making multisensory associations and even constructing symbols.

The European psychologist Martha Farah reported an interesting case of a boy named, rather appropriately, Adam, who at only two days of age contracted meningitis, an infection of the protective covering of the brain. Adam suffered temporal lobe damage and a resulting "face blindness" (medically, prosopagnosia)—that is, Adam's ability to recognize faces, a fundamental learning task of newborns, was severely impaired. At sixteen years of age, Adam continued to exhibit "impressively bad" facial recognition, as well as difficulty detecting visual objects. There are several important facets to this case: He was and remained significantly disabled in terms of visualizing faces, even though the damage was primarily temporal, that is, to the classical cerebral auditory, or *hearing*, area of the brain, and not to his cerebral visual area, where visual images like faces would be predicted to be stored.

Subsequent MEG and fMRI studies have demonstrated that facial recognition learning, in fact, occurs in three steps, phases, or stages: First, the learning event is roughly categorized in the right temporal (hearing) and parietal (general data storage) areas. Second, the memory is associated with emotions and body feelings in the thalamic gateway. Third, individual identification and storage—meaningful visualization verses just seeing—occurs in the occipital (visual) area in association with frontal (metacognitive) areas.

Adam's case illustrates that newborns are able to record data; associate the data with other data, emotions, and feelings; symbolize and give the resulting information an interpretation, and even "think" about it metacognitively. That is, they use multiple neurosensory inputs; they associate multiple, even simultaneous, learning object-data; and they use more than one brain area during learning. Finally, learning areas in the neonatal brain would appear to be quite adaptable (the technical term is plastic). Adam was, after all, still able to recognize faces and objects with difficulty.

SPEAKING UP AND OUT

Between seven and nine months of age, several important changes in learning processing take place. ERP and fMRI studies show that stylized babbling begins with the infant moving the *right side of the mouth*—that is, the left side of the brain (motor nerves cross over, left cerebrum to right body side and right cerebrum to left body side). This left cerebral predominance appears across all cultures, and reflects that a new kind of specialization and learning process is occurring within the infant's brain.

Brain-imaging studies demonstrate this shift to a left-sided cerebral predominance for *both* speech and hearing. On the other hand, nonlinguistic tasks like sucking and eating use both sides of the mouth, and the left side sometimes predominates.

Lateralization, as this process is often called, demonstrably co-occurs with multisensorial processing. Have you ever, in response to some rather simple question, caught yourself responding, "Yes, well . . . ah . . . ah" and oddly could "feel" the answer "on the tip of your tongue," but couldn't quite spit it out? Known as the McGurk Effect, after describer Harry McGurk and partner John MacDonald, fMRI studies demonstrate the mental struggle involved in identifying the right memory when information, usually from multiple brain areas, conflicts. For example, a person seen mouthing the nonsense syllable "GA" while one hears "BA" would commonly be interpreted as "DA." In more complex and emotionally charged situations, "tip of the tongue" and even sensorimotor breakdown can occur. Similarly, PET images of deaf adults fitted with cochlear (hearing) implants showed unexpected activity in their right occipital (vision) cerebral area. It is as if the brains of hearing-restored deaf adults were also *visualizing* the sounds in a manner much like lip-reading.

Although more experienced than newborns, infants still can't tell us in words what they're experiencing. Still, the above suggests that learning in infancy as well as later learning involves not only multiple senses, multiply associated areas of the brain, and considerable flexibility or overlap, but also a lateralization of functions between right and left sides of the brain.

GETTING THINGS STRAIGHTER

It's more than a bit complicated how a ten-month-old's mind sees sound, but look at the areas of vocalization and the varied brain functions involved. Infants slowly (or quickly, if you're a parent) narrow their primary focus to that of sound and visual saturation (cerebral functions). They begin to display a predilection for pattern, rhythm, and intonation (cerebellar functions). They even develop sidedness interference (a hemispheric cerebral and cerebellar function). What's more interesting, all of these appear at about the same time.

Also at about ten months of age infants begin babbling in their own "culturally" distinct way. Advanced imaging studies demonstrate a near-simultaneous increase in brain area specialization and speed of processing that corresponds with dedication and anatomic insulation (the medical term is myelination) of major groups of nerves in the nervous superhighways. This neurobiological analog of the "first words" experience so delightful to parents brings to an end the first, almost totipotential developmental period, and represents a "set course"—a body-mind commitment to speech, visualization, and the basic neurosensory motor functions. That which is learned and frequently used is firmwired. It is not so fixed, however, as to be a true "point of no return," as we shall later see.

Just as cerebral learning is firmwired at this time, so, interestingly, is cerebellar learning, in this case, creating for each of us our own unique basic learning templates and rhythms—in my opinion, the very "essence" of language.

It is the start of the "linguistic immune system," an internal ruler that will be used to decide what is "us" with regard to language and deserves our conscious attention and what is "not us." Before we utter our first word, our distinct, sociocultural mother language—its very dialect, tonality, tonal patterns, and inflections—becomes, to a large extent, fixed within us. This fixing changes our focus—it focuses our senses on what we need to know in order to learn more. The learning patterns acquired during this first period set the stage for all subsequent learning by establishing a "reference" point for deciding whether our subsequent learning events are natural (reaffirming) or interesting (unusual).

Learning during this first period is intimately commingled with our other emerging senses, emotions, and inner-body feelings, establishing a veritable "safety envelope." Within this envelope, "normal" learning (traumatic or not) will selectively take place. Learning inside this safety-zone is reaffirming or interesting; learning outside this safety net is internally redefined as traumatic, thus embedding and to a large extent fixing the birth trauma within our very bodies in the form of repressed "body memories," as they're sometimes called clinically.

It establishes within each individual a sensory-motion-internal feeling or sensory-kinetic-based "body-mind music." Around the time of Socrates, the ancient Greeks intuited that a unique relationship existed between physical motion, called "dance," and our physical world, perhaps one of the most exciting "new" areas of learning research. The end of this particular development period literally defines, by default, who we are fated to be.

A DELICATE DANCE

It's been shown both clinically and in brain-imaging studies that children from twelve to eighteen months of age commonly utilize associations to learn. For example, they can frequently be seen to shape and utter newly learned words without emotion—a tip-off that they are not able to fully associate their own internal feelings or emotions with learned motor acts. On the other hand, after eighteen months of age the association of object-data and investiture of actions with feelings and emotions is well documented. What new neurobiological forces drive learning during the second developmental period, and how exactly is this done?

My experience as a pediatrician indicates to me that infants are either born with or rapidly acquire interest and ability in using *tools* to assist in their learning. I can only make an educated guess at this point. It's still a bit like counting the number of angels that can stand on the head of a pin. However, I feel fairly comfortable talking about at least four, and perhaps five, tools of the mind that seem *clinically* present in the very young.

The newborn's ability to visually fixate on and mimic adults is a strong sign that babies are actually using adults as learning tools. Virtually all of the baby's birth reflexes could also fall into the tools category. For example, pointing and word-based verbal communication, emerging around a year of age, have been interpreted as attempts to control others, and control requires tools. Similarly, a fourteen-month-old's obsession with getting what it wants is a tool of sorts.

Imaging from fMRI data shows that these phenomena correspond with a fundamental shift from temporal-occipital to temporal-occipital-frontal activity. According to these studies, frontal areas of the cerebrum "focus and direct" a baby's conscious attention, and assist in changing short-term memories into long-term ones, or at least direct their storage. To do this, it is assumed that these frontal areas are involved in higher-level informational indexing, sorting, storage, and recall. The frontal areas, for example, light up on imaging when a learner is actively integrating or dealing with personal, social, worldview, and/or spiritual metacognition.

Frontal activity after two years of age seems involved in determination of novelty (roughly through ascertaining differences by comparison), generation of expectations, and comparison of learned neurosensory and sensorimotor data in the past and present. TMS and rTMS studies suggest that the frontal hemispheres specialize according to positive or pleasant right frontal, and de- or repressive negative or unpleasant left frontal associations.

There's a considerable body of accumulated imaging evidence that points to these frontal areas as essential to effective development and utilization of at least two of the most profound human tools, language and higher mathematics, quite probably a third (kinesthetic or internal body language), and possibly even a fourth (internal time consciousness). This may well be the basis for what we have come to know as the "body-mind-spirit continuum." In their most primitive form, the frontal areas have even been implicated in unconscious, or repressed, pheromonic communication.

I would now like to turn from the cerebrum to the cerebellum—the seat of rhythm and time. Recall for a moment that it is the cerebellum that directs control of fine-motor coordination, a principal learning focus during this period. Learning how to manage rhythmic elements of actions—sequencing, timing, duration, strength, intonation, and pitch—is what early cerebellar learning is all about.

In fact, fMRI studies indicate that perhaps as early as four months of age, the cerebellar hemispheres begin acquiring and storing rhythmic and time-sequenced sensory information. Accomplishing this task—that is, discriminating between rhythms, rhythmic patterns, and various time sequences, and then committing the data, associations, symbols, and interpretations to both short- and long-term memory, on the other hand, appears a herculean effort, compared with reflexive and object-data learning.

Like the conductor of a symphony orchestra, the cerebellum assembles and directs what is stored within the cerebrum, diminishing or even silencing some, while emphasizing or featuring other patterned sensations, responses, and behaviors. Clinically, four-month-olds are already practicing precisely timed vocal interactions with adults. The fact that they don't yet have enough cerebral "notes" indicates that early cerebellar learning occurs as a result of the dancing rhythmicity of dialogue, rather than through traditionally held devices such as vocabulary, grammar, or structure. When was the last time you heard a parent say to an infant, "No, no, no! How many times have I told you: Subject BEFORE verb!" or "Remember, 'i' before 'e' except after 'c'!" while cuddling it in their arms?

The classical linguistic elements of language are prerequisites to neither language acquisition nor effective communication! Small wonder that the starting "age" for primary education keeps slowly moving down, with educators and parents barely able to keep up with their expressions of amazement: "Who would have thought such a little child could learn that?"

At around two years of age, PET, MRI, and fMRI images show the cerebellum undergoing distinct lateralization. Children's brains engage their cerebellum whenever semantic tasks like reading, with or without overt articulation, are encountered. Furthermore, imaging studies show that consistently active, neural superhighway fibers of the cerebellum are being constantly favored for myelination. Use defines the functional mind. "Couch potato fibers" are gradually culled, rerouted, replaced, or displaced. *Imaging is on the verge of definitively demonstrating that the cerebral, cerebellar, nerve superhighway, and thalamic gateway systems need to be robustly interconnected in order for effective learning to happen.* Some PET studies are beginning to indicate that humor also helps children at this stage learn. Jerry Lewis, professor emeritus, please stand up and take your bow!

OPENING THE LEARNING FLOODGATES

PET studies at all ages show the thalamic gateway system to be intimately involved in attention arousal, subconscious emotions/feelings, somatic (body) sensations and memory, body-mind learning, and yes, you guessed it, effective traumatic learning. All indications are that the thalamic gateway system discriminates, attenuates, intensifies, and injects emotive elements into the major neural superhighways connecting the cerebrum, cerebellum, and body. This creates countless opportunities for associating

nerve impulses, hormonally mediated emotions, and internal body sensations (feelings) with other learning data, associations, symbols, and interpretations. What is learned in this manner is then itself subject to physical
change induced by unusually strong or continued neural, hormonal emotional and feeling states.

Current fMRI evidence, in fact, suggests that thalamic gateway-related
emotive data may in fact be *necessary* to move cognitive short- and mid-
term memory into long-term memory. This process is thought to begin
with a form of scanning—called "fast mapping"—of the neurobiological
data associated with a learning event, that finally "pops up" into conscious
memory. These "tools," typically discovered at one to two years of age,
progress through the stage of maximal brain activity at about three years
of age. After age three, it's all downhill.

According to recent electroencephalographic (EEG) studies, the thalamic gateway system may play an even more global role in learning. It appears that the thalamic gateway system has the ability to synchronize and
impress a generalized mental rhythm (called alpha, beta, and gamma
background activity) onto data, associations, symbols, and interpretations.
These background mental rhythms have the power to determine general
levels of consciousness from conscious wakefulness to semiconscious-
ness (for example, when a smart child is daydreaming) to subconscious
rapid eye-movement (REM) to unconscious REM sleep. All of these
states are associated with learning. PET studies further indicate that inspiration, creation, imprinting, memory culling, and physiochemical nervous system restructuring (for example, myelination) occur during each of
these states respectively. PET studies performed when subjects are wak-
ening from sleep suggest that the thalamic gateway system is directly involved in reestablishing consciousness, while interconnected cerebral
frontal areas are involved in focus, learning alertness, and consciously directed learning.

There are now integrated medical-imaging studies showing that the
thalamic gateway system is inseparable from circulating hormone and
pheromonic production, as well as sensation and effect (pheromones are
biochemicals secreted externally by an organism that convey information
to members of the same species—like those new "can't say no"
pheromonic perfumes you've probably heard about). There is some
(though less convincing) evidence from neuro-electrical studies that the

thalamic gateway system may help synchronize predicted and experienced information, but this function is also felt to be performed in the frontal areas of the cerebral cortex. It is, however, known now to be modulated, at least in part, through action of the biochemical dopamine. At this point in time, however, our biochemical understanding of learning has barely begun.

MRI studies confirm gradual and controlled progression of insulation—myelination—of major-use nerves from roughly two through fourteen years of age, a period often referred to by clinicians as the "latency" period. Children during this period are rapidly developing and deploying learning tools to help learn. Their learning style recognizably approaches that of their parents and playmates. Their energies are strongly directed at acquiring information and controlling their environments in a manner that is at least outwardly adultlike. During this period, females as a group are particularly engaged in developing tools of language and social interaction; males are similarly engaged in voyages of physical exploration, though this is by no means true for any one individual.

During latency, the progress of nerve dedication through myelination is measurably observable using brain-imaging technology and techniques. It is possible to document rapidly increasing, lateralized brain area dedication, and the faster neural transmission times associated with nerve myelination. This period, which many parents experience as the most idyllic of childhood, comes to abrupt closure with the onset of puberty.

Sometime between ten and sixteen years of age (females as a group, about two years earlier than males), a period of increased growth associated with sexual maturation occurs. Brain-imaging and neuro-electrical studies together show that during puberty, this neural dedication results in global reorganization. As during the neonatal period, myelination and thereby neural dedication are considerably accelerated. Experimental studies indicate that this major "final" period of reintegration and re-sculpting of the brain and nervous system occurs in association with rapidly rising levels of sex hormones.

So what have we learned? I'm hopeful that during this somewhat wild and wacky foray into medical-imaging studies, you will come to recognize with me that imaging studies further show that most of our past and current "fashion" of teaching and learning theories aren't all wrong, but they are narrow, often tangential, glimpses of the broad panoply of the brain's actual neurobiological learning processes. Without an understanding of the neurobiology of the brain, how could they be anything else?

The field of neurobiology is at this very moment rewriting whole new chapters on what, how, when, and where we acquire data, information, knowledge, wisdom, and truth. If nontraumatic, effective learning can be said to exist, then it must take a form different from what we currently know of teaching—beyond our current concepts of intelligence, genetics, wisdom, and even spirituality—a true shock to our current teaching-learning system.

Whether effective learning occurs traumatically, is related to the birth event, or occurs differently in males and females, or whether it occurs in a physical form within the brain as well as in the body, is not really the question: They do. If we stop and think about neurobiological learning as we now know it from clinical, anatomic, and imaging studies, we are no longer obliged to follow the path we have blindly trodden for over 2,000 years. Neurobiology counterintuitively refutes our entire contemporary teaching system. The maxim "Sit down, be quiet, listen, and repeat after me" just doesn't work anymore. It never really did, but in relation to our overwhelmingly traumatic learning experiences, society, institutions, and individuals simply refused to see that.

Imaging, the Rosetta stone of neurobiology, continues to develop and needs to become standard intellectual fare within educational institutions. It needs to be afforded the opportunity to be acquired, understood, and slowly permeate every fiber of our society, institutions, and individual beings. For that to happen, parents, teachers, students, learners, societies, and political as well as spiritual leaders will have to be willing to strive to acquire this "new" knowledge. What exactly constitutes this "new" knowledge? It all boils down to a better understanding of our physical selves and how our brains actually learn. Neurobiological understanding is neither a wish, hope, nor dream—it's a necessary part of being a parent, student, or professional educator, and a requirement for humanity to eventually step outside violence and into a state of true, volitional learning. It's a different world altogether—one in which humankind is offered the reins to our evolutionary development, by wresting them from trauma and, quite simply, taking them back ourselves.

Ultimately, neurobiology teaches us that we are the owners and captains of our own lives—that ignorance and violation are no longer valid excuses to defect from that responsibility. We have seen that ignorance and violation simply perpetuate the current system of traumatic learning and violence within our society, world, and spirit. Effective learning is not something that needs to be done—it is continually being done, with or without neurobiological knowledge and wisdom. As two of my mentors, Andy Anderson and William Martin, often said to me, it comes down to three simple words: "Just do it!" Our preparation completed, the stage is set, the curtains raised—it's time for neurobiological learning to begin to reveal itself in earnest.

Chapter Seven

The Neurobiological Way

I spent a good number of hours looking at mechanical images of people's brains, and yet, as interesting as they are, there's still a huge chasm between the image and the person. Slowly piecing together and improving our knowledge of neurobiological learning is, in a world immersed in trauma, functionally pointless . . . unless. Unless there is some form of effective learning that can free us from the tentacles of traumatic learning. If this can't be found, what's left are interesting clinical "war" stories, bunches of pretty colored images, and the pathetic appeal of simply another mental prisoner inescapably trapped in a living, traumatic hell.

THE WAY OF FLESH

Do you remember a song about John Henry—"the steel drivin' man"—and his hopeless battle against a machine? Critics of physically based approaches to learning often raise the issue of the "soullessness of mechanistic approaches" to learning. Well, hey! I agree wholeheartedly that it is discomforting to have to utilize machines to extend our senses in order to penetrate into our very souls. Letting go of ideational fantasy, our primary birth trauma defense, is more than unsettling; it's downright frightening. Actually, it can be little else, since our very first experience with contemporary reality *was* deeply traumatic and indelibly fixed the power of traumatic learning within not only our brains, but our bodies, minds, and spirits. In order to proceed, we will have to undergo an exorcism—replete with anxiety, fears, and dread. Initially it's a dark and lonely journey going back to our birth trauma and staring it in the face—seeing it for what it is and how it controls us. It's more than a lesson in neuroanatomy or neurobiology. Soon we'll see that it's a question of survival.

It's also easy to obsess about the "ghost in the machine" and completely miss the unfolding, not of another ideological "revolution," but of a neurobiological evolution. This isn't human-ape stuff. I'm talking about a real progression of our human souls—a new kind of freedom we have never before had at our disposal, and the awesome physical, emotional, intellectual, societal, and spiritual responsibilities that come with it. Software, firmware, hardware, and artificial intelligence are slowly penetrating every aspect of our world. Remember the fear that they would take over our world? They haven't yet; instead, our world has changed and adapted to their presence. I believe that the same will be said of neurobiological learning as we "boldly go where no one has gone before."

The above comparison between the processes of computerization and neurobiological learning is more than what it may at first appear. I believe that an understanding of how we work inside will prove considerably less than our fears of machines would have us believe. Neurobiological learning grabs our information age, and by acknowledging the role of bioelectrics, association, symbolism, and our own almost machinelike primary reflexive learning, it creates a physical and intellectual bridge between the two. These processes can then become free to produce new associations, symbols, cognition, and metacognitive discoveries, but they are always expressed physically. Thanks, Isaac Asimov!

Beyond this, however, the similarities quickly turn into differences. That is because, despite our greatest android fears, biological systems like ours have an inherent structure, organization, and function unique to themselves.

WHO, WHAT, WHEN,
WHERE, WHY, AND ESPECIALLY HOW

In the late 1800s perhaps the most apparently mechanical learning system of all time was discovered and reported. It was dubbed "conditioned reflexes" by Pavlov and others, whether applied to man or animals, and involves introducing two or more temporally associated sensory stimuli during any motor event, like ringing a bell at the same time that some mouthwatering food is presented. Eventually, just the sound of a bell ringing will cause the mouth to water. If you have a pet, you've probably seen this when your pet hears the sound of the electric can opener. You've also probably experienced it for yourself if you're trying to break a bad habit, such as smoking. With established or hard-to-break habits, if *any* associated stimulus (in the case of smoking, the right social situation, such as seeing a hot, steaming cup of coffee or smelling the early morning air) occurs, the linked motor or thought is automatically initiated (lighting up, opening the fridge, barking at a full moon).

Pavlov's findings regarding conditioned reflexes are just as true for humans and animals today as they were in the 1800s, although Pavlov didn't provide much for man's higher-level cognitive functioning. For example, humans, unlike animals, may continue to be motivated by a stimulus a long time after it was first presented. Dogs won't work very hard for an abstract "A," let alone one that takes three months to earn.

In the early 1930s and 1940s, Lorenz (the man whose brilliant discovery of imprinting was so readily adapted by the Nazis) identified what later came to be recognized as a special form of the generalized, conditioned reflex. Consider, for example, a reflex initiated between birth and early infancy that is specifically associated with a primary caregiver. This particular kind of reflex appears to be even more highly persistent. As I mentioned earlier, associations and interpretations, whether learned or impressed (an arguably fine distinction), are made more effective when *a mentor* is included. Notice I said mentor, not teacher or interlocutor. Is this distinction really that big a deal, though? You'd better believe it!

Business has long known of the power of imprinting. In fact imprinting is so powerful that linking a product with an image, touch, sound, taste, or smell through human demonstration—classic "advertising"—has become the very heart of business. Imprinting has grown in importance to the point of becoming a contemporary societal issue regarding what exactly humans learn about sexuality and violence while watching television and movies.

In the 1960s, Piaget and Montessori extended Pavlov and Lorenz's findings specifically to children. Later, the eminent experimental psychologist Alison Gopnik, in her groundbreaking 1999 book *The Scientist in the Crib*, clarified that at "lower" stages, phases, or levels, learning tends to occur unconsciously or semiconsciously. That is, object-data recording, along with association, symbolization, and interpretation, occurs largely without thinking. "Higher" stages, phases, or levels of learning, like cognition and metacognition, on the other hand, occurred consciously. But even more interesting, *there seemed to exist a second learning pathway, based on curiosity, discovery, and mentorship, that progressed through the same basic stages, phases, or levels as traumatic learning but was voluntary, volitional, and nontraumatic.* And this wasn't just a crack in the seemingly impenetrable world of traumatic learning; it was an alternate learning universe—one based on the same, universal neurobiological learning processes as effective traumatic learning!

At about the same time as Gopnik published her book, the honored biologist-educator Robert Sylwester, in his books *A Celebration of Neurons* (1995) and *A Biological Brain in a Cultural Classroom* (2000), began accumulating classroom evidence of what appeared to be additional steps, phases, or levels in effective learning. The game was truly afoot!

Most recently, Robert and Michelle Root-Bernstein, in their book *Sparks of Genius,* described thirteen "thinking tools"—observing, imaging, abstracting, recognizing patterns, forming patterns, analogizing, body thinking, empathizing, dimensional thinking, modeling, playing, transforming, and synthesizing—expanding the list of stages, phases, and levels of neurobiological learning as well as learning tools and again, most importantly, exploring further the nature of nontraumatic learning. You will note that the first three "tools" are quite similar to the three steps, phases, or levels of lower neurobiological learning; the next four involve the cerebral-cerebellar-thalamic gateway; the last six are attributes of "higher" learning.

RUDE AWAKENINGS

It remained, however, for the now-famous biologist-turned-anthropological linguist Terrence Deacon, in his 1997 book *The Symbolic Species*, to formalize what I consider to be the first inclusive neuroanatomical description of learning and the beginnings of neurobiological learning as I have described it.

From these contemporary geniuses, we find that there exists a second front in learning. At its core are two exceptional types of what, for lack of a better term, I call *symbolic learning*. The first is the "pop-up" (or "pop-out") phenomenon—you know, where you suddenly recognize a friend's face in a large, otherwise nondescript crowd. Popping up or out has been observed clinically and experimentally to begin appearing at about the time when symbolic learning, a variety of interpretation involving replacement with a simplified form, is being established—at roughly one to two years of age. In more "mature" clothing, the pop-out phenomenon results in the classic exclamation "Eureka! I got it!"

Second, there is the phenomenon of "explanation" itself—aptly represented during the "terrible twos" with "Why . . . Why . . . Why?" questioning. Symbolic learning is an important sidestep from traumatic learning steps, phases, or levels. For a curious toddler, it leads to seemingly unending explanation by association. Unending, that is, until it is suddenly capped by a popped-up or -out symbolic interpretation. Once again, the key here is not so much the existence of the phenomena, but that they appear to occur outside the classical traumatic learning pathway.

Based on my own clinical experiences, I think there are *three* lower levels of learning: object-data (indexical-iconic), associative (transitional), and interpretive (symbolic). These three levels correspond anatomically to (1) distinct point-areas in the cerebral and cerebellar cortices corresponding to neuro-electrical object-data, arranged roughly into lateralized temporal (hearing), occipital (visual), and parietal (multisensory) areas; (2) vertically arranged conic or cylindrical areas of interneuronal associations located between the cortex and additional layers containing neural superhighway and cerebellar-thalamic gateway neuron interconnections; and (3) deeper, variable, plate-shaped areas, where synchronized neural electrical activity occurs and can rapidly spread throughout the brain. It is most probably in this deeper, third layer where precognitive, symbolic meaning appears and is held.

Symbolism, at its inception, is a "lower" (often non- or semi-cognitive) stage, phase, or level of learning, but it also represents a major nexus—a learning milestone common to both traumatic and nontraumatic learning and also a point of critical divergence between these two learning pathways. Clinical and experimental findings as well as neural imaging studies seem to correlate well with the three lower neuroanatomical levels of learning I have described, and correlate with my clinical observations on lower-level subsequent language acquisition in trauma survivors.

This new construct, symbolic-level learning, and its attendant pop-out phenomenon, constitute the foundation of not only a new learning pathway, but an entirely new, nontraumatic learning theory grounded in neurobiology. In educational terms, this foundation, which is physical in nature and demonstrable in the clinic, laboratory, or diagnostic imaging center, is fully testable. And like eidetic recall, object-data; emotions; feelings; association; symbolism; absent, false, and ritualized memory; the paradoxes of traumatic learning and recall; the stability of traumatic memories; frozen and unfrozen survival learning reflexes; body-mind memory; rhythmicity; recruitment-reinforcement; lateralization; displacement; the roles of the cerebrum, thalamic gateway system, cerebellum, and the major nerve superhighways, as well as interpretive recrafting and recovery—all have physical, neuroanatomical correlates.

What can we observe from this new "three-lower-stage" learning vantage point? Neuroanatomical data are consistent with embryological, pre- and postnatal, infancy, and childhood developmental studies. They account for and provide physically based explanations for the phenomenon of peripheral learning. They fit our observations regarding the critical role of hearing and vocalization. They correlate well with critical developmental learning periods. They begin to shed light, albeit as yet incompletely, on the existence of alternative learning pathways, and they open the door to effective, nontraumatic learning. They even fit the spiral-cyclical nature of learning as it seems to occur within the human brain.

These three (or four, if you count symbolic learning as entirely different from interpretation) stages, phases, or levels of learning, however, cannot be all. There must exist "higher," conscious-cognitive steps, phases, or levels of learning, reflecting in some physical way the individual metacognitive, social, worldview, and spiritual stages, phases, or levels of learning. Explaining, in physical terms, the "higher" cognitive functions—cognition itself if you will—is the final challenge in our voyage toward discovering a single, unified neurobiological theory of learning. It's nonetheless a daunting challenge, so hold on to your hat while we catch the wind for the final leg of our journey.

IT'S A WIDE, WIDE WORLD OF INTELLIGENCE

There seems to be considerable interdisciplinary discussion and reasonable agreement among clinical, experimental, and brain-imaging studies with regard to the lower levels of conscious awareness. Perhaps this is because Freud already visited the area and began the process of chasing away the goblins under the bed. But if my observations are correct, there is substantially more to learning than either Freud's "id" and "superego" or individual awareness.

Since the most substantive of what we are learning about these "higher" thinking functions comes from clinical and imaging studies, I was quickly forced to confront one of my own prejudices: I had to figure out what it meant to say something was "true" when the brain said so . . . and why my own biased brain should be trusted with this very important task. A problematic topic that once again immediately became apparent was the issue of "intelligence."

As I mentioned earlier, there are lots of "intelligent" people out there (or for this discussion, perhaps I should say "highly educated") who seem very sure they can test for and measure intelligence. The fundamental problem is that all the work so far with intelligence, to my mind, hasn't even resulted in an adequate definition yet, and surely intelligence *must* be something more than the ability to demonstrate some particular strategies and techniques, or to perform some highly gender-biased developmentally linked "tricks" at the proper chronological age.

Another way of approaching this problem is to say that if teaching is, in fact, an extension of Platonism in which ideals exist within the minds of the teachers to pass on to students, and in which students can be tested for intelligence, then surely there must be some kind of common agreement as to what constitutes Truth, the highest of the Platonic ideals. Unfortunately, this is not at all the case.

A few decades ago, this question was not *physically* resolvable—more evidence of our need to enter boldly into a search for neurobiological awareness. Recall for a moment the Triune Brain Theory. Such ideational brain constructs represent physical truth, right? They should, or what's the point?

Well, the answer is yes. And no. And yes. Yes, their existence implies that a truth does exist in the mind of the teacher (and soon will in the mind of the student, if the teacher has anything to say about all this). No, most of our current teaching ideas do not reflect physical reality with regard to the brain, let alone show how it actually learns and what it actually knows about the physical world. Yes, like rats on a sinking ship we don't stand still with our ideas, but rather run from one to the other, hoping that we will find in this frenetic process one that will not sink beneath critical clinical, experimental, or nowadays brain-imaging scrutiny before the entire ship sinks.

More than 2000 years ago, Plato, the first "Teacher," acknowledged this problem with ideals. He likened the mortal human struggle to "see" the truth to prisoners in a dark cave who can see only shadows of the real world being cast on the wall before them. All we ever see, chained in the dark cave of the real world, are shadows of reality—shadows of the truth. Only an enlightened teacher knows the "real" truth. Is that it? If there is a "real" truth, is there, then, an "unreal" truth? And, I'm sorry, but according to this analogy, it seems to me more likely that teachers would simply know, at best, a different, same shadowy truth. Teachers can't agree on a definition of intelligence that fits physical reality—and that definitely smacks of a shadow on the wall of a common cave! Is there then simply no answer to so basic a question as to what truth is? Or, stated another way, why are there so many different answers? If neurobiological theory fits reality, it should also fit the unseeable ideal, in this case truth and intelligence, better than other theories. Or, at the very least, it should have something useful to say about them—something useful that we can grasp, hypothesize about, create experiments about, and test.

In working through this book, that is, addressing effective learning in terms of traumatic learning, we have actually been applying neurobiological theory and method in order to ascertain it—we've quite literally become educated beyond simple data. Intelligence, knowledge, wisdom, and truth . . . that's metacognition in a nutshell. When we discover what intelligence really is and is not, we will clarify some of the most profound issues that exist about the "learning tools" of truth. What is the neurobiological nature of cognition and metacognition? How do they come about? How are they maintained, crafted, sculpted, and destroyed in neurobiological terms? Does higher learning follow one or different neurobiological pathways? What about the natural course of evolution of neurobiological learning? Can we direct it ourselves?

FOX OR HOUND?

The greatest difficulty with defining and measuring intelligence is assumed to be a simple matter: We just haven't yet found the right "solution." Another way of looking at it is that we just have to wait for neu-roanatomical knowledge to catch up. The first is a sort of "rats abandon-ing ship" scenario, the second like, trying to hitch a free ride on a bus. I believe the problem is more general and complex; I believe it involves a lazy definition and an odd, patchwork approach to measurement. "No, no! It's those vacationing neurons," I can almost hear some readers saying. OK, then, let's look at all three.

Historically, educators have persistently taken an ideological rather than a physical approach to the definition of intelligence. Call it job inse-curity. So what would a particularly intelligent definition of "intelligence" be? Well, first it should be based on the neurobiology—physical aspects—of learning. It should at least be consistent with what we know about hu-man learning. And one thing we know about learning is that while it may begin from the same "big birth bang," it quickly diverges in such a way that it doesn't work exactly the same in males and females. I say it "may" begin with sexual equality—but, while both male and female fetuses are continuously bathed in essentially the same maternal pregnancy hor-mones, sexual differentiation progresses from such a *very* early point that I wonder . . .

Another thing we know is that humans go through distinct develop-mental levels, reorganizing their neural systems accordingly. A third thing we know is that accidents happen. Learning occurs. Sometimes what hap-pens is intrinsic, like misfollowed genetic instructions, and sometimes ex-trinsic, like asteroids crashing into the earth. More commonly they're mixed traumas—effective learning events and acts—that change not only what, but how we learn and think.

Most intelligence tests end up relying on comparisons of verbal, visual-spatial, and mathematical answers between the individual being tested and groups of "normal" individuals of similar chronological age. It's assumed that intelligence is something more than the answers themselves. By ap-plying statistics, intelligence will somehow "express" itself. By this rea-soning, intelligence should be the same for equally intelligent males and females, and should remain the same over a lifetime. Theoretically, if con-structed well, intelligence tests should be capable of measuring intelli-gence in similar species, like apes or dolphins.

Critics of these tests argue that the opposite is true, saying current intel-ligence tests reflect a person's moment-to-moment smarts—the amount of social and cultural preparation they've had in anticipation of the particular test problems. As for asking an ape or a dolphin to do a standard intelligence test, well . . . Sadly, I eventually came to agree with the critics: The intelligence tools I was using to work with patients and students just weren't working very well. In fact, over time it became clear that intelligence quotients, or IQs as we commonly call them, were to be believed or disbelieved based on whether the results seemed to fit the situation.

In fact, most intelligence tests are impossible, or at best very difficult, to administer to animals, newborns, or infants. I am always awed at the arrogance of humans "proving" that humans are intelligent (by definition or by the fact that they can and are willing to be subjected to testing) and all other animals are dumb (they couldn't and generally won't take the simplest of human intelligence tests). Maybe the lack of animal intelligence as we see it is more indicative of our arrogance and lack of intelligence in being capable of either defining or constructing physically based intelligence tests. After all, the ability to smell like a dog (and I mean to pick up a scent, rather than to have one) is a finely tuned skill quite comparable to the visual skills measured as part of "intelligence" in a human.

In my experience, uncorrected intelligence scores even differ between male and female humans, and they change as test subjects become more or less "skilled" with learning tools for their age. Interestingly, I have looked intensively for, but have yet to run across, brain-imaging work on either "photographic memory" or intelligence. This is, perhaps, expressing one of my own pet peeves against the lack of depth in defining intelligence. Unfortunately, or perhaps fortunately, depending on how you look at it, my pet peeves are not the only problems with intelligence. The wider problem is that we simply don't know what we don't know about intelligence and its measurement. The smartest dog doesn't laugh at a "Far Side" cartoon (maybe he's too smart to), while people laugh (in itself, an odd behavior indeed) at the "stupidest" things!

The idea of intelligence has not translated well into physically related measurements. Writing and "higher" mathematical skills (higher than numeracy, or what we commonly call counting), for example, are purely imaginative inventions. In a way, that's what makes them "intelligence" tools. Testing these ideological inventions is like Alice looking back into another looking glass: We end up testing tests, and then testing tests of tests, and so on. And what if what we have invented in our minds is quite simply wrong? You see, intelligence doesn't fare well in a world of Platonic ideals either. It is even more of a phantom than Plato's shadows!

Most intelligence tests measure something representative of ebbing and flowing cleverness. Most *IQ* tests *test* vocabulary, verbal ability, clarity of expression, visual-spatial recognition and/or manipulation, abstract mathematical ability, reasoning, ability to use tools, creativity, curiosity, sense of discovery, intuition, insight, inventiveness, cognitive clarity, conscious presence, judgment, habit, use of age-appropriate exploration strategies, ability to explain, developmental maturity, grounding, awareness of "truth," rhythmic awareness, even "kinesthetic thinking" (some football players, for example, demonstrate real backfield genius). At one time or another, some combination of these attributes has been considered one and the same as intelligence. And (shades of linguistics!) none measure either medical or language acquisition intelligence. These seem like two major omissions to me.

Another criticism of intelligence tests has been their seemingly innate gender (or sex-hormone) bias. According to David Wechler, Alfred Binet, Theodore Simon, and William Stern, males consistently received lower scores than females. Of course, my wife assures me that this is not surprising and argues strongly that such a test is quite valid. In the process of reading this book, we have seen that these differences interestingly parallel differences in gender development. Boys experience slower overall development over a longer period of time than girls. There have been many so-called "anecdotal adjustments" to IQ tests to "correct for gender bias." But what exactly does that mean? Such adjustments, in fact, are not any better than my holding on to whatever intelligence measure "correctly" reflects what I see clinically. It's a sort of Machiavellian zero sum game. Ultimately, the problem is that the tests simply don't come out consistently the way we want them to. You may well laugh at this, but it is simply another kind of truth! Unfortunately, the "adjustments" have served to lend credibility to IQ testing itself, and they have been generally embraced by the business of American education. When they agree with what we need, they are most handy. When they don't, they are simply overridden.

But let's assume, for the sake of argument, that there now exists some form of "gender equality" in these tests. The appeal here is mostly based on societal ideational objections against invidious gender inequality. Neurobiology, however, is ignored in order to use these tests to advance societal and political ambitions. Here's where IQ equality bogs down in ideology. Neurobiology, on the other hand, establishes that there *are* differences between genders, and so neither "side" needs to figure a way around it.

There are five indigenous neurobiological flaws with our current IQ tests. First, females actually do rely more heavily than males on language to acquire knowledge and solve problems. Second, while females are exploring their world though talk, males are relying more on their visual and tactile skills. Third, males tend to visualize the world more in terms of movement of static objects in space, an ability that is important in abstract mathematics; females (as a group) score consistently lower in these areas. Fourth, intelligence tests are difficult (if not downright impossible) to administer to the very young. Finally, scores steadily decrease after adolescence, implying that animals, newborns, infants, and our "wisest" elders lose or lack intelligence. These limits are neurobiological realities. What mystifies me is why we haven't used neurobiology to try to resolve these problems.

A move toward neurobiologically relevant categories will prove helpful in developing a better intelligence test. For example, some of the earliest versions of a neuroanatomical intelligence recognize at least two "kinds" of measurable, physical intelligence—"fluid" and "crystallized." On the other hand, both clinically lack a much-needed (and sometimes overriding) cognitive component. They are, like the triune brain, just too simplistic to account for what is actually going on in the human brain. If they are not enough, then where should one turn?

I don't claim to have the definitive answer. But I was forced back to 1904 and the pioneering work of a brilliant engineer-turned-psychologist, Charles Spearman. In his seminal works, *The Nature of Intelligence* and *The Abilities of Man*, I witnessed an interesting sort of "Bill Gates meets Freud" scenario unfold. Spearman, quite simply, believed and provided some interesting evidence for a dimensionless core intelligence measurement he called the g-factor.

THE G-FACTOR

In 1904, Spearman declared that he had found a way to measure "core" intelligence. Best of all this measure would give a fixed, nonvarying measure, independent of age or gender, in the form of a single number. Spearman called this measure general intelligence, or "g." Interestingly, a g-factor can be calculated for almost any combination of test items, subtests, or tests; however, a g-value with consistent, significant correlation(s) is established almost exclusively only when dealing specifically with mental tests. Despite (or maybe because of) the controversy that it has fueled, g remains one of the more controversial studied intelligence measures.

The g-factor has been variously described as "the common factor," a sort of universal translator, and even a common "thought language," a cognitive abstraction, attention, mental energy, or a measure of neural plasticity. Controversy centers on how any single intelligence measure can reflect the structural and functional totality of as complex a thing as the brain. After all is said and done, g is like the bone that's left after a very thick soup has boiled away, and the mathematical abstractness of a unitless number is nothing short of staggering.

Spearman, interestingly, anticipated many of the concerns I have just mentioned regarding conventional IQ tests. Who would want to switch an unreliable test for a more complicated, unreliable test? No, the point is that g seems to work, and it addresses some if not most of the real-life clinical, experimental, imaging and, in general, neurobiological factors we have been discussing. For example, studies have demonstrated that g doesn't improve with experience or training; g can account for mild mental retardation and late social, educational and even, to some extent, occupational outcome; g appears genetically determined; and finally, g represents a cognitive age not aging cognitive expression. But to me, one of the most significant characteristics of g is the way growth through age fifteen or sixteen is not just accounted for, but quite accurately predicted. Then, at around age sixteen, intelligence definitely ceases. That was a joke (just testing to see if you're awake). What I mean is that g even reflects how intelligence seems to change and vary after puberty. Thereafter, g normally remains at a maximum level, unaltered, right up to the end of life (barring, of course, injury, physical trauma, or disease).

From a clinical therapeutic viewpoint, g is a factor in virtually all sensory-based hearing, and in most vision. With the exception of tactile tests, g seems to fit what I have clinically observed regarding neurobiological learning—what works, like music, space, higher mathematical reasoning, symbolism, and most motor skills, as well as what doesn't, like counting. But these hardly represent the sum total of the learning processes I have uncovered in my own practice—processes that include, for example, "lucid dreaming," directed dreaming, meditation, and *déjà vu*. Spearman himself anticipated several other independent, "universal factors" than just g and s (non-g-factors), including will (designated "w") and cleverness ("c"), as well as "perseveration" and "oscillation."

AND THE WORDS MAKE FLESH

Interestingly, "g" appears to be independent of language usage. This means we may even be able to answer the age-old debate: Who really is smarter, the owner or the pet? Another way of saying this is that language is not really a primal form of intelligence. Instead, it is another learning tool. This may be the sought-after key to understanding gender bias within current intelligence tests. It is, after all, primarily in the selection of learning tools that men and women differ.

Spearman's critics have argued that g may be a mathematical artifact, more a deceiving shrink than a missing link. My opinion is that g fits the clinical, experimental, and brain-imaging data incredibly well, given that we came to much of this new knowledge eighty years after Spearman's work was published. I think Spearman was prescient in separating intelligence from tools, and cognitive abilities from consciousness. Many of my conclusions about neurobiology owe a debt to Spearman. Clinically, I suspect there are four degrees of g: reasoning; its close counterpart (and often confused cousin) logic; truth; and consciousness.

OURS IS NOT TO REASON. WHY?

Most people, if asked what reasoning is, would reply, "Reasoning is using logic." (Thanks, Mr. Spock—Live Long and Prosper). But reasoning in a neurobiological sense is much more than pure logic, and has many facets, for example, symbolic, perceptual, and linguistic logic. Actually, these are quite different, perhaps even more different than similar. The great news is that humans, even children, do reason. Younger children appear to reason mainly through trial-and-error strategies. Older preadolescents reason using anticipatory strategies. Adolescents are capable of reasoning by calling on formal strategies (though it often seems to the "older" generation that they either don't use their reason at all, or are perhaps aliens from another planet using some form of logic incomprehensible to their surrogate terrestrial parents).

Reasoning has been increasingly identified in the literature as a neurobiological tool based on clinical exceptions to the rule as, for example, in the case of schizophrenics, for whom reasoning seems to break down. Clinicians sometimes see abstract reasoning breakdowns in Fragile-X Syndrome males at or near adolescence. This, I am betting, will prove to be another interesting case of sex-hormone-related differences. PET, fMRI, and other brain-imaging studies will be required to unravel these kinds of exceptional situations in which reasoning appears to be affected in order to understand the nature of reasoning. "Beam us up, Scotty! Scanners on maximum, phasers on stun!"

Logic itself is slowly becoming distinguished from reasoning based on PET and fMRI studies. Clinical and experimental data taken together suggest that humans possess at least two separate neuroanatomical forms of reasoning: deductive (*à la* Sherlock Holmes) and inductive (like Albert Einstein and his famous equation $E = mc^2$). While both are accessible, after puberty the predominantly left-sided deductive function should be more accessible to males, while the inductive advantage should go to females. Males, when challenged, do better at (and prefer to do) higher mathematical reasoning; females prefer linguistic or language-based reasoning. So, ladies and gentlemen, it is literally true that asking for help from your spouse actually does "get on his (or her) nerves."

While Broca's (listening) and Wernicke's (speaking) areas are commonly located in the dominant (left if you're right-handed) side of the brain, language information and logic appear to "lateralize," going to one side of the brain or the other, quite early. Generally speaking, visual-spatial information scoots to the nondominant hemisphere along with visual-spatial logic, context (e.g., jokes), rhythm, pitch, and emotive content, implying that these factors might be of special importance in deductive reasoning. For myself, I should like to find out if traumatic learning is lateralized, and if it is processed differently by males and females, perhaps at the metacognitive reasoning level. Both types of reasoning, deductive and inductive, appear subject to learning and even relearning. It seems likely to me that both are under continual development pressure in animals as well as humans. It would also be interesting to investigate lateralization, if any, of hormonally differentiated learning in nonhuman animals. Just what was my dog thinking when he gazed quizzically into my eyes yesterday?

Living and practicing in Hawaii, I have had the good fortune of seeing repeated instances of learning differences by culture. Perhaps just underneath the Asian cultural influence, a different sort of logic and reasoning is emerging. James A. Michener, in his book *Hawaii*, seemed to think so. Eastern Asians may be creating pressure to develop an "emerging" third type of reasoning, combining deductive and inductive reasoning into a new, holistic hybrid.

It seems likely to me that "female"-driven, inductive reasoning may be closely entwined with language development, and perhaps be vital to second-language development. It is just as likely that male-driven, deductive reasoning may be pushing the visiospatial frontiers of language, like for example written logic.

Whatever learning results from reason and logic, neurobiology is playing for large stakes. No matter how differently our sexual hormone systems are driving the collective development of logic and reasoning, there's one goal we all share: We all seek external validation of the results of our logic and reason by "testing" it, again, against the truth.

TRUTH OR CONSCIOUS CONSEQUENCES

I have tried to make a compelling case against ideational or "ideal" intelligence, the kind that teachers have been unsuccessfully pursuing for centuries. I have also tried to make a reasonable case for physically based intelligence—in this case, through reference to "g" as a possible way to solve the riddle of intelligence. I hope you can at least agree with me that reason and logic are tools that human males and females both use in order to learn, though in fact we may use them quite differently. This finally takes us to the closely related issue of neurobiological truth. And truth seems to be what consciousness—"higher" learning, metacognition—is ultimately all about, isn't it?

Once again, the answer is yes—and no. Clinically speaking, symbolic thoughts, like interpretations, being noncognitive, have no absolute "truth" value. That is, unless given meaning through conscious reason, logic, social, worldview, and/or spiritual analysis, development, and explanation—justice. You see, justice, not truth, creates the neurobiologically felt sense of truth. Justice is almost always expressed within a particular explicit or implicit context. Justice results in truth that can be checked against contexts, external or internal—our choice. This may sound like a purely semantic argument, but it's not. There are big differences, I think, between Platonic (ideational, teacher) and Socratic (physically based, neurosensory, neuroanatomical, neurobiological, learner) truths. The former may turn out to be truly true or not; the latter are always true. The biggest difference is that neurobiological truth is neither eternal, unchangeable, nor perfect. It is, in fact, temporal, changeable, and grounded in feelings (a felt sense of justice) based on individual, social, world, or spiritual metacognition. So . . . wham, thank you, that's it. Like it or not, this is where neurobiological learning—our brain—ultimately leads us. I never said it was pretty. But it's physically real. It's rooted in the dust from whence we came. It is what makes us human.

While this may be the bells, whistles, and fireworks of contemporary neurobiological learning, it is not the end. No, I believe there's much more yet to be revealed. One area I am especially cognizant of, working with trauma survivors, is that neurobiological truth doesn't necessarily change the world or make what was learned ever go away. Learning, after all, is part of our experience, our metacognitive self. But it does result in wisdom, a holistic, felt sense of self-trust. Remember my conclusion that things learned at the associative or higher level are *always* true, but true only in that they are selected and made to fit an individual's immediate needs, wants, or desires? Learning, at the cognitive and metacognitive steps, phases, or levels is soft and flexible as tin, and varies substantially from individual to individual experiencing the same learning event. Small wonder that teachers sense the need to be oppositionally rigid when they sense just how fluid "truth" is within our physical reality.

Justice (felt truth) and wisdom are, in fact, just metacognitively processed "body memories." They are what makes interpreted object-data feel and therefore *seem* "real" and "true." Amazingly, these physical sensations were known to the ancient Greeks—we'll explore these important upper-level attachments of body, physicality, and truth in more depth later. But for now, the sense of truth has some interesting characteristics of much more immediate consequence to learning. For example, we have to reconsider the learning truth in adolescents, children, infants, newborns at the moment of the great birth trauma, and finally fetuses, as what is learned during these developmental periods. These transient, developmental truths contribute keenly to all of our subsequent learning.

Over the years, my clinical work with children and adults indicates to me that truth is strongly dependent on one's developmental level. To an "outsider," this would seem folly. To a neurobiologist, this is totally reasonable. For example, clinically, until about four years of age, children have little to no sense of deception and have great trouble conceiving "untruths"—what adults regard as "real" lies. Children sometimes have a problem associating the right sources with their facts, and sometimes it is so severe that it creates a condition called "source amnesia." It is not at all uncommon for children, for instance, to confuse movie fiction with fact. Adults, on the other hand, are generally held responsible for their mistakes and their consequences. It is intriguing, though as yet not possible, to comprehend what a newborn thinks about the birth event, but I am eagerly awaiting this one. One thing I can predict, though: Based on what we know of traumatic learning in adults and children, and the neurobiological process, it is profound.

Early imaging studies were performed under a variety of conditions, and often involved unclear or even undefined object-data, associations, symbols, and interpretations. On the other hand, none of us are *always* clear in our thoughts or memories. As you might expect, much interest has been directed at recent tests conducted during intentionally inflicted deception and guilt. Some of these do and will continue to come from criminal court trials, injury cases, and victim interviews, but these represent notoriously difficult situations within which to run accurate tests. Few steal from the candy jar when being closely watched. Still, we do know there are reactions in several parts of the brain to what is actually or intentionally not true.

Unclear or conflicting information of any kind and at any level, when presented during brain imaging, appears to activate a specific area of the thalamic gateway called the anterior cingulate cortex, or ACC (think of the movie *Memento*). On the other hand, *deception*—for example, one person lying to another with the intent of having the person believe them—appears on fMRI to activate the frontal cerebral cortex (except, of course, when conflicting information is perceived, and then the ACC is also activated—think of the movie *50 First Dates*). Guilt—the act of deceiving—activates the brain globally (one might even say catholically), not unlike conditions when one is being asked to come to an intelligent decision. This brings us to speculate about the global capacity of guilt's counterpart, consciousness—the state of trusting belief in one's perceptions, at every inclusive stage, phase, or level, around a learning event.

I've obviously come to the point in my own mind where reasoning, for me, is clearly a neurobiological entity, quite separate from intelligence and truth. Interestingly, I am finding that imaging studies increasingly support the point of view that reasoning is a tool used to manipulate consciousness and metaconsciousness.

TIME AND YET AGAIN

There is a whole library's worth of information by philosophers, educators, linguists, biologists, and even physicians about thinking, consciousness, and cognition. These days, this is especially so in the fields of psychology, metaphysics, and artificial intelligence. The sheer volume of work indicates that "consciousness" is an elusive entity at best, and what's being written proves it. Neurobiologically speaking, there is extensive *indirect* evidence regarding its existence: Works can be found dealing with ecstasy, sleep, narcolepsy, sleepwalking, anesthesia, hypoglycemia, hypoxia, encephalitis, delirium, hallucination, schizophrenia, shock, electroshock, coma, near-death, and even death. Given the extent of the indirect literature, what can be said about it neurobiologically?

It appears to me that, like intelligence and truth, there is no one focal "seat of consciousness." It is possible, however, to identify distinct, widespread, underlying synchronized activity within the brain during periods of conscious, conscious perception (for example, awareness of the awareness of a sensation). Beginning between twelve and fifteen months of age, there exist at least two likely neurobiological consciousness pathways. The existence of two pathways, phenomenal awareness of self and metacognitive awareness, implies the existence of two states of self-awareness. The first, a kind of physical awareness, has been associated with increased cingulate area activity, an area demonstrated to be involved in resolving unclear or conflicting information (see the previous discussion of ACC). The second, as a whole, is less well-studied, but it appears that metacognitive awareness touches on personality often associated with precuneus and angular gyrus activity, almost always in association with cerebral cortical frontal area activity.

The precuneus just mentioned is a distinct cerebral cortical (conscious) subarea of the parietal (flexible storage) area of the brain located just in front of the occipital (visual) area and next to the sensory strip that senses the body's main muscle groups like the fingers, the mouth, and the legs.

The angular gyrus is another subarea of the (conscious) cerebral cortex, located at a point of juncture of the parietal, occipital, and temporal (hearing) areas. The latter has been associated with, among other things, "out-of-body" experiences.

An integrated or "full" sense of reflective self-awareness is said to develop when physical and personality awareness are active together, lighting up, as it were, much of the surface of the cerebral cortex of the brain. All involve what I have already described as felt sense.

There's also neurobiological evidence of temporal (in this context, I am referring to time, not cerebral hearing) awareness—more specifically, a sense of the passage of time, what I liken to a seventh sense (the sixth being kinesthetic or internal feeling). Where exactly does this sense of time passage come from? That is an especially intriguing and incompletely understood phenomenon. Brain imaging, using the fastest response technology and techniques, suggests that previously learned object-data, along with its attendant associations, symbolic representations, interpretations, and metacognitive meanings, are being constantly compared with "similar" recently learned object-data (along with their more limited associations and interpretations) and with "similar" immediately occurring learning object-data. These comparisons create a sense of past, present, and future. Of these three "states of mind," by far the most interesting is the future. Studies of future time sense, for example, *futur vu* (premonition), are most intriguing, and suggest that an additional phenomenon, "anticipation," is involved. During anticipation, associations, symbolic representations, interpretations, and even metacognitive meanings are transferred *in toto* to object-data with similar attributes that are now being sensed.

The entire process of time consciousness—temporal impregnation—reminds me of a modern action movie that jumps rapid-fire from one short scene to the next to build a powerful, almost surreal story line. From numerous imaging studies it appears that inside our brain, this amazing process probably goes something like this: In response to a new learning event, simultaneous object-data nerve excitations occur in their respective areas throughout the brain. This occurs against a background of generalized, synchronized, global rhythmic activity—the collective background of cerebral thought (object-data, associations, etc.) and cerebellar rhythmic consciousness. A quick event-background analysis by differences is performed to see if anything unusual is happening. If so, subconscious attention is focused on the event. If not, it is "ignored." Every four to 300 milliseconds, nerve impulses surrounding a significant learning event are resampled. A "ripples in the pond" effect is thus created as rhythmic thoughts are associated, interpreted, and symbolized until a pattern is abstracted, usually in the cerebral frontal areas. This temporal pattern is used to anticipate (predict) the immediate next (future) pattern and determine whether the event continues to be unusual—whether it's worthy of conscious (cognitive and metacognitive) attention.

During this time, the collective information and patterns being sent through the thalamic gateway, along with one's emotions, feelings, and hormonal status, begin accumulating and collectively resonating. If a particular threshold is reached, then, like a laser, the pattern bursts into medium- or long-term memory. If the particular threshold is never reached, the learning event remains in short-term memory and is eventually dealt with and "forgotten": It is not repressed; it is simply not recorded.

Returning back to temporal impregnation, analyses of differences between predicted and current patterns are performed in the frontal areas, this time collating the amplitude (energy) of their qualities, similarities, *and* differences. At this stage, amplitude includes any amplification (as described above) as the nervous impulses pass through the thalamic gateway. In response, a felt sense of either well-being or anxiety is generated based on the narrowness or wideness of differences, respectively.

I apologize if this explanation seems interminably long and complex. Actually, what I'm describing all generally happens in less than the blink of an eye (about 250 milliseconds). But it illustrates several important points: First, it is the process of repeated analyses of differences between past, current, and anticipated information that creates a felt sense of not only well-being or anxiety. Here also is our uncanny "intuition" or "premonition," when events we need, want, or desire to occur in spite of relatively wide differences do indeed occur. The tangibleness or intangibleness of sensed objects, as well as a felt sense of the passage of time itself, is also born here. In other words, it appears possible to explain, hypothesize, test, and even evaluate reality and time itself. What is more interesting to me, though, is the fact that reality and time, like truth, have more to do with what we need, want, and desire than with ideals. Having come this far, have you made the next leap of discovery? *There is, in fact, no need for Platonic ideals or teaching in a neurobiological world!*

Let's return yet again to temporal impregnation. The temporized firing patterns mentioned aren't sporadic. For all their seeming complexity (even to the point of appearing chaotic), they allow, support, and follow a sophisticated but predictable neurobiological learning pattern: object-data, associations, symbolic representations, interpretation, cognition, metacognition. I am not willing quite yet to argue that this entire "package" is itself encoded in a biological organism. *If it were, then the product would be normalized and integrated over time, much like a completed movie, in which flowing, rich meaning is created from a set of sequential, still pictures. The overall process is not unlike neurobiological learning.*

I think one might come to agreement, over the course of this process, with those who view human and artificial intelligence as similar. Completed thoughts become amenable to yet another step, phase, or level, this time of algorithmic simplification and encryption—"knowledge," I like to call it. If so, at this even higher level we may, at this very moment, be stumbling on *the essential, raw datum of neurobiological truth*—knowledge—and with knowledge of knowledge, wisdom itself. This again opens a door to explain, hypothesize, test, and analyze even more interesting phenomena. For example, I have often wondered about our felt sense of timelessness—is this the place from which springs a felt sense of eternity?

SLEEPING WITH DARWIN

I would like to turn for a while from consciousness to a most interesting state of unconsciousness: sleep. That sleep is important to humans is reflected in the fact that in spite of a strong drive toward consciousness, and an equally powerful fear of conscious dissolution—dying—we spend a third of our lives voluntarily, sometimes even appreciatively, relinquishing consciousness.

Sleep is associated with many important functions: bodily maintenance, memory, even myelin modification. These well-documented functions are not frills; they are necessary, as clinical and experimental studies of sleep deprivation and various sleep disease states have shown, to maintain integrity of the mind, body, and spirit, both individually and collectively.

Most intriguing with regard to my work, sleep is a "normal," regularly recurring, physiological state in humans, which *begins with the dissolution of consciousness.* Because of this, sleep presents an unprecedented opportunity for studying consciousness and metaconsciousness, and the particular contributions they make to effective learning. Investigating, for example, if and how learning occurs during sleep (a time of voluntary un- or at least subconsciousness), or during the stepwise reestablishment of consciousness upon waking, should yield important insights into the neurobiological processes involved in metacognition.

Contemporary clinical, experimental, and imaging studies, for example, using PET technology, repeatedly demonstrate that neurobiological (re)awakening progresses through distinct, discrete stages. First, there is a sudden reestablishment of "lower" brain stem, thalamic gateway, and specific, generalized, global, neuroelectric patterns and rhythms—much like jump-starting a car on a cold morning. Next, a specific area within the midbrain called the reticular activating system is initiated. Then activity in subareas of the front portion of the cerebral cortex associated with attention and alertness are resumed—as it "warms up," the car begins to run smoother. These processes are being defined in increasing detail even as I write.

What is most important here is that consciousness, cognition, and assuredly metacognition as well, like Freud's famous "ego," are not, as he imagined, a single state physically located in one specific area of the brain. Instead, cognition appears to be a stepwise process, not unlike awakening, and the result of the actions and interactions of many different areas located throughout the brain.

Cognition, on the other hand, is not amorphous—an idea like "ego" without pure physical existence. In fact, I hope at this point that you will agree with me that its physical existence is well grounded neurobiologically. These simple observations do not belie each other; they do, however, through their seeming paradox, using counterintuition, lead to some profound conclusions: First, cognition, because it is a stepwise, to some extent linear, process, is in itself temporal—that is, it would be expected to occur in a manner not unlike that of neurobiological time-consciousness, something already described in some detail. Second, consciousness and metacognition, because they involve rhythmicity, are, to some extent at least, cerebellum dependent (recall that the cerebellum is the source of rhythmic memory). Third, because cognition requires the interaction of multiple areas of the brain, there must exist some sort of physical coordinator—at the least, a set of instructions, perhaps a set of very primitive, learned reflexes. Imaging studies suggest that frontal cerebral area activity is crucial to the integration of these during cognition.

Imagine with me for a moment that such primitive reflexes as we posited above are probably instigated before birth—something not at all inconsistent with what we already know about cognition at or before "normal" birth—before the singularly important, traumatic birth event. In other words, is it possible that cognition is, in fact, itself learned, and subject to further learning?

If the steps, phases, or levels of learning so far described are, in fact, hierarchical (and are themselves learned and used in a certain order), then metacognition, the latest step, phase, or level of learning, should be the most subject to learning modification—which indeed it appears to be. Since metacognition appears to be present early, but is fully developed later in life, it might be the best place to start in a search for a nontraumatic form of effective learning. Might it be possible, for example, to nontraumatically modify or "adjust" what is learned at the metacognitive step, phase, or level? Can we, by our own volition, switch from traumatic to nontraumatic learning by partially altering the steps, phases, or levels of effective, traumatic learning?

My clinical work leads me to believe that personal cognition is that oh-so-elusive key to wresting control of our own learning processes, and beginning the long-needed transition from traumatic to nontraumatic learning.

This also leads us to perhaps the most fundamental and profound question: Are we ready to assume responsibility for our personal and collective development and, ultimately, evolution? Are we ready to let go of centuries of seductive, illusory ideations and to rely on our own intrinsic neurobiological processes to make this transition? Are we ready to let go of our childish but cherished ideas about time, truth, and even our traumatic ideations about religion, God, death, and the afterlife? If you are ready, that is, you are ready to let go of teaching and trauma—to instead boldly open your mind to learn and discover a new world of an entirely different form—then it's time to begin the next phase of our voyage.

NOT IN OUR WILDEST DREAMS

Shakespeare's Prospero, in Act IV of *The Tempest*, says, "We are such stuff, as dreams are made of . . ." Did Shakespeare know from experience that learning occurs during "normal" sleep? Neurobiologically speaking, we know that learning can occur during traumatic, frozen, trance, hypnotic, EMDR, and regressive states. PET-imaging studies of patients waking from coma or hypnosis show that they go through very similar waking processes. What we learn during sleep and sleeplike states changes not only our memories, but also how we see the world—our own consciousness, cognition, and metacognition.

Like a Mount Everest climber or a high-flying aviator learning during hypoxia (oxygen starvation), dreaming, strictly speaking, does not *have* to be un- or semiconscious. Clinically, I have helped patients become conscious, and to increase their consciousness during dreaming. This therapy, sometimes called lucid dreaming, can be used to change dreams and memories.

Lucid dreaming is said to occur when a person becomes aware that he or she is dreaming *while still in the dream state*. Folklore strongly warns us against lucid dreaming: It was said to be a time when we walked the netherworlds with ghosts and goblins, soulless and naked. Another belief was that when one awakened from lucid dream states, the normal process of bringing the soul back into the body would be interrupted, and the person would become a sort of walking dead—a zombie. This is a powerful sentiment to millions of people practicing voodoo and other forms of "witchcraft," in which it seems to work if you believe strongly enough. Neurobiological reality is not as morbidly appealing, but it is no less sensational. My clinical experience strongly suggests that lucid dreaming is a genuine though unique learning state bereft of metacognition—that is so-cial, world, and spiritual awareness—within which there seem to be no boundaries to one's self-awareness.

Techniques exist to assist in controlling and directing lucid dreams. Some lucid dreamers have learned how to successfully use vivid dream characters, much like avatars in video games, to activate learning. Lucid dreamers often describe these characters as infinitely more real than avatars. To many, they are so "real" that they can be asked and agree to perform and later even successfully accomplish tasks, both in the dream and in the nondream world. Drawing a picture, writing a name, naming some unknown words, finding rhyme words, or solving math problems are just a few classical lucid character tasks that have been clinically demonstrated. For some, their dream characters exercise or can be taught rational reasoning, a sort of first step in acquiring a consciousness of their own. When this occurs, dreamers, after awakening, often comment on subtle metacognitive changes that have occurred "on their own."

Lucid dreams can include visions of luminous areas of light, peripheral light, disks of light, or sunlike concentrations of light. Often, the disk appears to remain in a fixed location, even when dreaming body movement. More interesting, the location of the disk may be fixed from one lucid dream to another. Some physicians I know have reported that patients recalling near-death experiences and effective recovery dreams involve similar phenomena. It's been my observation that while communication between a lucid dreamer and his or her dream characters usually takes a nonverbal or verbal form, the character often speaks—uses language. These observations seem to be important and fruitful areas for further research into the neurobiology of cognition and metacognition.

It has been suggested that metacognition is a "higher order" of consciousness involving "thoughts about thoughts"—a distinctly human ability that heralds the successful transition to adolescence to adulthood. PET-imaging studies, however, clearly demonstrate adultlike metacognition as early as three years of age; this lower limit may simply reflect the earliest age when such studies have been attempted. There is limited clinical evidence of social metacognition as early as eighteen months of age. Contemporary PET, specialized EEG, and SPECT (a recent high-resolution enhancement of PET) show neuroelectrical activity virtually identical to that observed in other metacognitive states in adults at the youngest ages tested.

Metacognition reads like a spring weather report: It shows large-scale, synchronized, global activity with scattered and constantly changing points of activity in parietal and frontal areas of the cerebral cortex. I have found metacognition to be of particular importance in subsequent language acquisition. Similarly, an extraordinarily traumatic event is difficult if not impossible to describe without metacognitively redefining it ("It was like . . ."). There are, unfortunately, too few studies, even anecdotal ones, to fully define the neurobiological role of metacognition in learning. These areas, however, clearly deserve additional clinical, experimental, and imaging exploration.

While social- and world-viewpoint metacognition studies are few, there are a surprising number on spiritual metacognition! Before presenting further information, there appears to be a distinction between individual spirituality and participation in organized religion. The former is spiritual, the latter social; each, in my experience, exerts a different metacognitive effect. Both differ neurobiologically from "belief." Given this distinction, it did not come as a surprise that, on brain imaging, religious recitation of mantras evoked metacognitive-like brain activity. Religious delusions in schizophrenic patients, on the other hand, invoked a totally different brain activity pattern. For more details regarding imaging, spirituality, and religion, I recommend to you my previous work, *A Neurobiological Theory and Method of Language Acquisition*, as an excellent and contemporary place to begin.

Spiritual metacognition, including sleeplike meditative states and lucid dreaming, is volitional, intentional, and malleable. Noted educator Rachel Kessler, in her book *The Soul of Education*, fearlessly explores the role and use of spiritual metacognition in the classroom, mixing traditional teaching (traumatic learning) with individual, volitional, and discovery-based learning at the spiritual metacognitive level. Spiritual metacognition, whether violational or volitional, appears capable of affecting neurophysiological as well as long-term and permanent physical alterations in many, if not all, body organ systems. My clinical work suggests that spiritual metacognition is currently in an active state of development and evolution in humans.

It remains to be seen whether the various clinically identifiable steps, phases, or levels of metacognition (social, world, and spiritual) share different or common neurobiological mechanisms. My clinical observations lead me to predict that although invoking common neurobiological processes, differences will, over time, become more apparent than similarities, and that these differences will likely come more from the selective, volitional *inhibition* of various areas of the brain, rather than the activation of "new," undiscovered areas. Inhibition of activity in select areas of the brain during imaging studies is pathognomonic, for example, of the meditative state.

Further studies in spiritual metacognition should open doors to an understanding of inspiration, creativity, and other spiritual "mysteries." For myself, during the last several years, I have become especially interested in whether metacognitive processes are, indeed, steps, phases, or levels of learning or actually acquired, formal tools of learning, "equal" in importance with higher mathematics and language.

Chapter Eight

Neurobiological Learning

Our culture holds the brain in a revered place, sitting godlike at the top of our bodies, hidden inside the skull and largely not understood by the average person (readers of this book excepted). Have you seen the television anti-drug advertisement of a frying pan with an egg in it? If I remember correctly, as the egg begins to fry, the words "This is your brain on drugs" appear. The allusion is artfully inaccurate: Aside from being biological, the brain is not really much like an egg at all. We've spent considerable time exploring what the brain is; I think it is time to give some attention to what we now know the brain *isn't*.

WHAT THE BRAIN IS NOT

The brain is not a simple one-to-one, grammatical, or structural-rule-to-neuron system. It's not a raw egg, cooked in grammar, structure, discourse, psychological, social, or reconstructionist rules. A pity.

It isn't organized top-to-bottom or bottom-to-top or like a computer—quite irritating, really.

Its organizational and operational "logic" does not appear to be based on semantic, lexical, grammatical, structural, psychological, emotional, cognitive, or formal logic. Learning rules is not what neurobiological learning is about (downright exasperating)!

It does not begin at birth—at birth, it is neither organized by nor does it operate based on any universal grammatical rules, but neither is it simply an empty bucket, waiting to be filled. How galling!

Learning doesn't occur as one neatly developing process from birth through adolescence.

Early learning doesn't occur in the same way as adult learning, with one exception: Learning occurs in any possible way. Learning is like a rushing tide, sloshing advantageously through every crevice—once begun, it continues along whatever pathway is available.

Learning doesn't become more effective as the result of more repetition, instruction, teachers, classrooms, schools, syllabi, curricula, administration, or money. It's insultingly resistant to planning!

Learning is not the same for males and females—a gross transgression in a gender-equitable age like ours!

After adolescence, learning never returns to the "state of grace" experienced during infancy and early childhood. Regardless of the amount and quality of post-adolescent learning, actual intelligence itself does not increase—in fact, it remains quite stable until an accumulation of acquired neuroanatomical disabilities begins to sadly inflict a gradual decline.

Finally, natural, effective learning is deeply and complexly entwined with traumatic learning, both in content and form, but it can be volitionally directed to develop along an alternative pathway, that of curiosity, which utilizes many neurobiological processes common to traumatic learning.

We can ignore the neurobiological tenets of learning, but only at great cost to our individual and collective potential—and if that doesn't grab you, well, then, it takes up an inordinate amount of our lives and money.

WHAT THE BRAIN
(AND NEUROBIOLOGICAL LEARNING) IS

First and foremost, the brain is organized neurobiologically. This organization "makes sense" in terms of learning and explains effective, traumatic learning. In fact, neurobiological learning (NL) is necessary and sufficient to explain effective learning, and it is consistent with anatomical, clinical, experimental, and imaging information. While NL theory doesn't completely explain everything about learning, where it lacks, it provides sufficient material to create numerous, rich, testable hypotheses, each with promise of further extending the borders of NL and understanding. NL is soundly grounded in physical reality and does not require recourse to fashionable ideations. NL is sufficiently complete and robust as to underlie virtually all current ideational teaching and learning theories.

NL occurs in discrete steps, phases, or levels, beginning with object-data and proceeding through association, symbolism, interpretation, and cognition to metacognition and possibly beyond. It explains, again in physical terms, the various learning processes employed, and their limits throughout each of the currently recognized learning periods of life. These stages can be adequately described in purely physical terms, such as sympathetic nervous system stimulation, nerve myelination, and the effects of sexual hormones.

Semantic, lexical, grammatical, structural, and formal logic and reasoning can all be derived from, but do not explicitly determine, the development of the human brain. The rules come after the fact. This principle is a guiding force in NL.

Neurobiological learning probably begins closer to inception than birth. Little is known about learning prior to birth, but learning after birth is driven first and foremost by the raw power and form of the traumatic birth event. Within hours after birth, a second learning system, based on curiosity and discovery aided by maternal imprinting, begins competing with traumatic learning for precedence. Learning from this point on occurs in any way it can, bounded only by the limitations imposed by learning steps, phases, or levels; developmental periods; and traumatic "environmental" events.

Information appears to be stored, recalled, and utilized best when multiple, sensed object-data are associated together with emotions and feelings, grouped with other associations into symbolic forms, interpreted, and defined within a personal, social, world, and spiritual context. That which fits NL is best learned, and that which is best learned makes the most sense. Learned information is stored in the brain, when and where possible in proximity to other, similar, sensory information, which in turn statistically defines the general storage areas of the brain.

Neurons within the brain, whether dedicated or not, are constantly being organized and reorganized under the control of the frontal areas of the cerebral cortex. Because of this, learners can choose nontraumatic learning, and when they do, they retain the power to accept or reject teachers and teacher-ideas, as well as to choose learning resources and mentors within the limits of availability. In a similar fashion, mentors choose learners whose sensory abilities match (what I think of as "sensibility," in some instances to the point of sensuality). Choice is, if at all, a very late component of traumatic learning.

In traumatic learning situations, teacher-student pairings are stressful, involuntary, and usually limited by design or circumstances. In nontraumatic learning situations, mentor-learner pairings are nonstressful, volitional, and rarely limited by design, though to some extent by circumstances. Traumatic learning is almost always effective, although the majority of what is actually learned is unpredictable and almost inevitably includes many unwanted triggers and behaviors. Nontraumatic learning, when it is curiosity-based, discovery-driven, and mentor-supported, is almost always effective, and the majority of what is actually learned is predictable and rarely ever includes unwanted triggers and behaviors.

Traumatic learning is dependent on presentation, control, and how the teacher, usually orally, interprets what is happening to the student. Nontraumatic learning is dependent on learner resources, both internal and external, the learner's cognitive experience, and what the mentor demonstrates, not what he or she says.

The onset and length of periods of accelerated myelination, along with neuron use and power, determine what is "firmwired" and, in a way, constitute the beginning of the end of learning, at least with regard to myclinated neurons. Differing myelination "area-rate-preferences" ultimately lateralize brain functions in a different manner for males and females, giving each distinctive, nonoverlapping, intra-, inter-, and extragenerational advantages.

Hormones generated during developmental periods and traumatic, sexual, and transformational learning events have the power to amplify learning as well as initiate myelination. After adolescence, selective demyelination and remyelination still occur, but at slower rates for both males and females. Post-adolescent demyelination and remyelination are based largely on neuron usage and result in subsequent neural recruitment, displacement, pruning, and truncation in a zero-sum fashion.

While intelligence does not increase after puberty, neural speed, dexterity, metacognitive ability, and thereby learning continue to do so. Most important, however, is acquisition, recognition, familiarity, use, and integration of the sixth sense (internal feelings), the seventh sense (internal time consciousness), and possibly additional neurosenses associated with curiosity, cognition, self-discovery, and metacognition.

Finally, with effort, a learner can volitionally choose to transform learning from a traumatic to an alternative, nontraumatic process utilizing curiosity, discovery, and mentorship, which utilizes many of the same NL processes common to traumatic learning.

TRANSFORMATIONAL LEARNING—A BOLD NEW WAY IN A BRAVE NEW WORLD

"All our knowledge has its origins in our perceptions."

—Leonardo da Vinci

"Sit down before fact as a little child, be prepared to give up every conceived notion, follow humbly wherever and whatever abysses nature leads . . ."

—Thomas Huxley

"Every act of conscious learning requires the willingness to suffer an injury to one's self-esteem. That is why young children, before they are aware of their own self-importance, learn so easily."

—Thomas Szasz

"You cannot teach a man anything; you can only help him to find it for himself."

—Galileo Galilei

"Who questions much, shall learn much, and retain much."

—Francis Bacon

"You don't understand anything until you learn it more than one way."

—Marvin Minsky

"[That] you have learned something . . . always feels at first as if you had lost something."

—H. G. Wells

"When the student is ready, the master appears."

—Buddhist proverb

REBEGINNING

Like most other "new" German school physician-educators, I am by nature skeptical. I try hard not to buy into purely ideational hocus pocus, irrespective of how intriguing or inviting it may be. I try to keep my mind open, clinically use what consistently works, critically examine every exception to the rule, and trust in what I can physically sense and experience.

I have repeatedly witnessed individuals embarked on a voyage of curiosity, discovery, and transformational learning, with the help of a mentor, "thaw out" and transform even the most frozen of traumatically learned, self-destructive, acting-out behaviors. If one understands the neurobiological processes involved, one can effectively self-regenerate—redefine, or heal, as it were—even that which was taught and learned traumatically. Careful now, I didn't say *get rid of* the traumatic experience—what was experienced, especially traumatically, will always remain with the learner. It becomes, in fact, an inseparable part of the learner's being.

The experience—*what it means, and the way it effects our ongoing learning process*—can be changed. I have had the privilege of seeing crippling "old" traumatic memories and beliefs loose their grip, allowing the learner the freedom to once again return safely to that precious childlike state of curiosity from which transformational learning springs, revisiting and further redefining the trauma within a new context—that of new life instead of the darkness of misery.

This transformational form of learning is quite different from traumatic learning. Transformational learning (TL) is volitional, curiosity-based, discovery-driven, and mentor-assisted, and does not seem to carry with it the unwanted triggers and behaviors that accompany traumatic learning and fit so poorly in nontraumatic situations. TL can occur at any step, phase, or level of learning, but it seems particularly effective at the "higher" cognitive levels. It can actually restructure history, meaning, and truth as we now know it. In order to achieve effective, nontraumatic, transformational learning, "teachers" must refrain from teaching and instead become willing to demonstrate, at all times, the TL process *in their own lives*. In addition, both mentor and learner must be willing to let go of the concept of ideal truth, and be willing to tolerate the prediscovery discomfort and frustration that inevitably precedes discovery.

Let me say that another way: The measure of a good teacher has always been that his or her students learn not only effectively, but also with ease. Classical teachers teach students by their actions and attitude that learning is easy. "See, look at me! You may feel inadequate, but I have everything at my [mental] fingertips!" If this isn't the case, then the student isn't studying or learning correctly, and should abandon the effort and go find the teacher again (of course, it could also be that the teacher isn't teaching and managing the classroom correctly—the old "whose fault is it?" teaching-failure conundrum).

My own clinical observations in conjunction with the clinical, experimental, and imaging evidence presented by Gopnik, Kessler, the Root-Bernsteins, and countless educators, teachers, and tutors, on the other hand, show that what I call transformative learning occurs as the result of mentor actions and attitudes that learning—discovery—is rarely easy. It is, at best, discomforting, especially just prior to discovery. When learning feels uncomfortable, TL reinforces learner persistence, until discovery finally pops up or out. Transformative learning, in fact, occurs entirely within the learner, without the assistance of a teacher (teachers are often said by learners to "get in the way" of transformational learning).

In addition, transformational learning offers two additional and entirely unique rewards over traumatic learning: knowledge and wisdom. "Truth" becomes intimate to the transformational learner; depends on learner needs, wants, and desires; and is no longer a divine pronouncement of the teacher's ideational reality. That is, transformational learners develop within themselves *their own* process and yardstick for lifelong learning.

The complex interweaving of data, associations, symbols, interpretations, personal cognition, and social, world, and spiritual metacognition involved in effective, traumatic, and transformational learning is neither simple nor actually far removed from its instinctual reflexive roots. From the clinical vantage, effective traumatic learning, which we have used to forge the foundation of transformational learning, has provided us with a primitive, catalytic place to begin our exploration—a sort of learning matrix map.

Neurobiological learning and its nontraumatic form, transformational learning, are actually not *about* teaching or truth. Teaching is traumatic; truth is an illusion. What they are about is acquiring information about the world through our senses and feelings, and experiencing that truth within.

In the process of neurobiological learning, each learner begins with the widest range of learning choices possible for any given situation. This is what makes both traumatic and transformative learning so exceptionally effective. Ultimately, in its applied form, transformational learning is about understanding the basic tenets—the "natural laws"—of neurobiological learning and the role of mentorship in effective learning.

THE SEVEN NATURAL LAWS
OF TRANSFORMATIONAL LEARNING

Getting professional educators to be more open-minded about NL, and not just continue to talk the ineffective talk of teaching, has proven a far more difficult task than I had ever imagined. As early as 1923, Charles Spearman, the "g" man discussed earlier, eloquently voiced this impasse. Psychology, and psychologically based learning theory and methodology, "has in modern times so degenerated as to become scientifically unusable" (Spearman 1923, p. 21).

Spearman stressed the importance of developing both theory and methodology directly from "natural laws," that is, tenets derived from physical rather than ideational data. Every time I read this, a light flashes in my mind, and I immediately begin to think of the whole of what is known about NL—clinical, experimental, and imaging—in terms of its basic tenets. What exactly are the "natural laws" of neurobiological theory and method, and transformational learning?

The physical evidence speaks strongly in favor of the existence of a single underlying, unifying theory of neurobiological learning that in its application follows two pathways—traumatic and transformative learning. Once this is accepted (and I hope at this point that I have garnered your agreement), the challenge becomes one of applying this general, neurobiological learning theory, in terms of a common method or methodology, back to learning as it actually occurs. On careful reflection, NL methodology, and thereby transformational learning (TL) methodology, seemed to me to spring from fifteen "natural laws" or tenets of effective learning, described in detail in my previous book, entitled *A Neurobiological Theory and Method of Language Acquisition*, and summarized here in the form of seven fundamental tenets.

The First Law

Learning that is particularly effective, efficient, and stable can, does, and should be assisted to occur.

Effective learning *can* be forced to occur . . . this is the very essence of traumatic learning. Traumatic learning, though highly effective, results in unwanted learning with myriad attendant, often crippling, liabilities. In its transformative form, neurobiological learning is, first and foremost, "allowed" to occur. Allowed neurobiological learning can be assisted — strongly facilitated, in fact — by the presence of a trusted, and in the best case, experienced, mentor, one willing to *experience with the learner* and show his or her process of curiosity, discovery, self-discovery, and metacognition, wherever the process may lead. It is through demonstration rather than explanation that TL, and thereby effective nontraumatic NL, occur.

The mentor's responsibility to encourage transformative learning is not trivial. Once a learner is fully engaged in the transformative learning process, the process rapidly becomes persistent, self-recruiting, and self-reinforcing. In a sense, a mentor's main responsibility is to make sure that the learner comes to no harm . . . trauma. Given the biological nature of learning, I have been pleasantly surprised at how closely this parallels the same physician's primary responsibility under the Hippocratic Oath. In practical terms, that means avoiding and, where necessary, extinguishing traumatic learning.

It's hard for one traumatized person to help another. All of us carry information distorted by early traumatic learning. Unresolved traumatic learning is often carried into (the clinical term is "acted out" within) relationships, including relations between students and mentors. A mentor must be ever-vigilant for traumatic reenactment, neither engaging in nor refusing to engage in, but rather constantly "letting go" of opportunities to "act out" the learner's or mentor's past traumas.

In fact, a personal sense of student and mentor safety is essential for a strong mentorship relationship to develop. By its very existence, mentoring creates an invitation for learners to reenact past traumatic learning experiences. The drive to do this is both primitive and powerful. Consider, for example, a student who has been physically traumatized around some learning event — caught in a traumatic, neurobiologically learned stimulus-response pattern from the past — involving a trusted parent. A strong and safe mentorship relationship will provide an opportunity for the student to reenact the old trauma in an attempt to transform it: "See, the perpetrator-teacher was actually the exception to rule because, in a similar situation, my mentor didn't act the same way. *Most* people would have acted like my mentor." Reenacting old trauma, however, while infinitely seductive, is not conducive to transformative learning. It seems like it should be, but it isn't. Why?

Traumatic reenactment rarely transforms what was learned traumatically. Instead, it usually reinforces what was traumatically learned by creating an *additional* and very compelling traumatic learning opportunity. The higher fidelity the reenactment, the more likely that some portion of the trauma itself will be unwittingly reenacted. In a play where the players aren't aware of their parts, reenactments of any of the triggers (even, for example, feeling anxious when a similar summer breeze brushes one's face) end up reinforcing the original association or new, unpredicted, traumatic associations. The result is actually a new, stronger, even more complex and extensive traumatic response pattern. This is not mentorship; this is a desperate appeal for exorcism—a situation every mentor must be attentive of, and that must be referred to a therapist to unravel.

Sadly, I am finding an increasing number of such traumas associated with failed teacher-student interactions! I am not one who enjoys pointing fingers, but I feel it's necessary to say something here about school violence: Teaching itself is violent in nature, and schools present a perfect stage for traumatic reenactment. Few people want to acknowledge this; it's just too painful for students, teachers, and parents alike, all of whom have at some time or another experienced that trauma, and are now involved in its perpetuation. Given this situation, I have been repeatedly asked what social form neurobiological learning, if broadly adopted, would naturally invoke. I believe it to be the ultimate fulfillment of distance learning. That is, resources, including evaluation, would be provided by institutions over a distance to local learner-mentor pair groups. This "new" form of education would end both school and teaching violence. It would bring learning back under family control and within the extended family unit. This is a change so profound that it will require a subsequent work to more fully address. And yes, it has already begun.

Ultimately, it is always the mentor's (or in the classroom or school, the teacher's) responsibility to be both aware and wary of traumatic reenactment and its inevitably destructive consequences. I have often speculated about the impact of the suicide of Socrates, Plato's mentor, upon Socrates' students. Was Plato's establishment of the very profession of teaching, of schools, education, and ultimately the business of education, a reaction to this overwhelming trauma? I wonder. Denying the consequences of effective learning doesn't diminish the power of its effects.

The Second Law

Effective learning persists, is self-recruiting and self-reinforcing, and has profound physical and moral consequences.

Neurobiological learning, in either its traumatic or transformational form, is highly effective, often persisting throughout a learner's lifetime. Transformationally learned information appears more open to change, especially at the "higher" (personal, social, worldview, and spiritual) steps, phases, or levels of learning.

Both are self-recruiting, but through different neurobiological mechanisms: Traumatic learning is subject to compulsive reenactment through a desire for *repetition of the traumatic learning event*. Transformational learning, after discovery takes place, is accompanied by a feeling of physical release and the release of endogenous opioids, an "intellectual high" much the same as an athlete's high, creating a desire for *repetition of the process*.

Again, while both are self-reinforcing, the processes involved are somewhat different: Traumatic learning creates myriad undesired, inappropriate object-data-emotional-feeling associations, each capable of being triggered. When triggered, they reinforce the original traumatic learning event. In a sense, they become "crystallized" within the sympathetic nervous system as well as the brain, and their effectiveness is enhanced by this and any accompanying discharge of stress hormones. Transformational learning, on the other hand, creates myriad appropriate, "everyday" associations, frequently reexperienced during our daily lives, which, like a growing web, reinforce each other. This is the very heart of holistic, nontraumatic learning.

Imagine for just a moment, what Genie, the Los Angeles "wild child," learned about people, society, the world, and her God, strapped in her potty chair for ten years and being beaten for making any noise, or Arthur, while he was the subject of traumatic learning experiments. How will they reconcile what they have learned with what they will experience after the trauma is over? Clinical and experimental studies confirm that neurobiological learning actually changes the way the brain is structured. It is not unreasonable to assume that traumatic and transformational learning, each involving common neurobiological elements but in different ways, would result in gradually diverging personal, social, worldview, and spiritual universes—divergent evolutionary paths—each constantly competing for their particular physical and moral existence within each of us, as well as within humanity as a whole. Perhaps this represents, in the words of Neil Armstrong when he set foot on the moon, the next "small step for man, one giant leap for mankind."

The Third Law

Effective learning can be implemented in virtually any setting.

Classical teaching occurs primarily in the classroom. Neurobiological learning occurs in any setting. Classrooms are an essential part of the contemporary "business of teaching," yet they are neither necessary nor sufficient for effective learning. The ascendance of teaching—and classroom management, orderly control, and rows of desks and chairs facing forward toward the teacher—is being assailed even as I write, by a worldwide diffusion of learning through tutoring, homeschooling, electronic interactive learning, and distance learning. This particular tenet frees students from the inanity of "seats of learning," and sets neurobiological and transformational learning free from the tyranny of the classroom.

Educators and "teachers" are increasingly acknowledging that the nontraumatic learning that occurs in the classroom commonly occurs in spite of it. NL theory and methodology addresses something infinitely greater than today's hallowed "business of teaching": They address learning itself. The illusion that classroom management is a door to efficient and effective nontraumatic learning is, quite simply, bursting its hinges.

The Fourth Law

Effective learning begins with peripheral introduction of learning objects, and it is strengthened by sensory, emotive, and kinesthetic associations, resulting in rich, symbolic interpretations of what was learned.

The effectiveness, efficiency, and power of neurobiological and thereby transformational learning aren't based on repetition or drill. We have seen that learners do not necessarily learn more from repetition. In most instances, more is less. The obsession of traditional learning with the repetitive introduction of fixed, centralized objects is counterproductive—drill blunts the brain's opportunity for the most lasting kind of understanding, peripheral object discovery. Even more importantly, it robs the learner of his or her volition—one's basic dignity.

In fact, as we have learned, after the first few centralized repetitions, humans and animals are prone to extinguish the learning object from sensation, perception, and consciousness. Could this be why so many children these days must be drugged in order to tolerate teaching in the schools? At the least it explains why the brightest minds wander inattentively, daydreaming, eventually letting the frogs loose. Drill is traumatic—the pain of it and much of its potential is repressed even as it occurs. Even as centrally focused traumatic learning takes place, the learner begins unconsciously creating myriad unwanted neurosensory associations, setting the stage for further trauma and traumatic learning.

Effective neurobiological learning begins peripherally and is brought repeatedly, by choice and through the learner's own energies—as a result of curiosity—into central focus. It begins with sensation and grows, like ripples in a pond. As object-data, feelings, and emotions associate, the whole becomes symbolically represented and interpreted. Finally, meaning is assigned, personally and within a social, world, and spiritual context. Typically, attention is first drawn to differences in high-contrast edges and rhythmicity. These typically stimulate a learner to consciously and repeatedly bring the object into the center of physical and mental focus and to begin the process of effective neurobiological learning.

The tendency for learning materials to "fade" from our center of perception may be as important as helping students "keep" new data. A central topic or theme of interest to the learner, for example, student dating, is acknowledged. The learner is then given tools to centralize peripheral learning objects like unusual spoken prepositions or a new discourse marker. The learner must centralize the peripheral learning object (expending energy and committing it to memory, so to speak) even as he or she is moving what was in the center of attention to the periphery (focusing curiosity momentarily on the newly centralized learning object). The second learning step, phase, or level, that of association, begins even as the central and peripheral learning object-data are being juxtaposed. The newly centralized learning object is instantly reinforced collaterally. This reinforcement is in the form of other co-occurring peripheral sensory object-data (especially sensations), feelings, and visceral kinesthetic sensations (kinesthetic sensations being the most powerful). Learning at this stage, especially when associations are sparse, slowly fades, and despite any felt sense of realness, falls subject to misinterpretation.

The next step, phase, or level of learning, symbolization, is more than just a higher level of learning. As Deacon points out, symbols represent a radical shift in neurobiological learning strategy. Groups of symbols, for example, can be transformed into "chunks" of information. If powerful enough, or if accessed frequently enough, the neurons involved will eventually receive an "insulation wrap": they become wrapped in myelin—"myelinized"—and become functionally dedicated, in effect, "firmwiring" them into particular symbolic memories and memory-enmeshed tasks, a process nothing less than amazing!

The Fifth Law

Auditory-visual and visual-spatial-rhythmic symbols are usually the learner's first learning tools. Self cognition and metacognition are quantitatively measurable learning levels available to learners in mid-adolescence and beyond.

Most educators acknowledge the importance of neurosensation in learning. Some espouse the singular learning role played by listening and visualization. But few are aware of the fundamental role that rhythm plays in learning. Whether the learning is traumatic or transformational, rhythm and rhythmic patterns—music, especially when accompanied by movement, dance—are the glue that holds object-data, associations, symbols, and interpretations together. Without rhythm, there would be no structure to learning. It is so important that the body has a second brain, the cerebellum, replete with left and right cortical hemispheres, dedicated almost entirely to rhythm and, in the broadest sense, the musical dance of learning and life.

The first three or four steps, phases, or levels of learning are often erroneously referred to in the literature as "short-term" memory. But they actually occur against the panoply of physical *development* through post-adolescence. These dual complexes are of particular significance, for example, in primary and subsequent language acquisition. Taken together with the effects of sex hormones, neurobiological development can be roughly summarized as follows: Cerebral and cerebellar learning begin well before birth. The thalamic gateway is strongly activated during the birth event. Establishment of cerebral cortical learning areas, along with myelination, peaks at about two years of age. Brain cell numbers are predominantly established by age six. Brain cell growth peaks from six to twelve years of age. The neural superhighways are "fixed" by age fourteen (they are still alterable later). Brain-cell-size growth begins to slow at about eighteen to twenty years of age.

Myelination plays a particularly important role in extending the processing power of the brain at virtually every level, and also in attaining critical capacity. There seems to be a "critical mass" necessary to shift the "higher" levels of learning, such as self-cognition, metacognition, and quite possibly less well-understood ones that, for example, respond to longer cycles like the reproductive cycles, or even supercognitive functions, into high gear. These higher, more conscious steps, phases, or levels of learning are attended by increasingly complex frontal cortical activity in the human brain. Individually, they are not more powerful than the "lower" levels of learning—in fact, they depend on them—but taken together, they substantially augment the learning process. Most importantly, they are levels of learning that continue to develop well after closure of the critical pubertal learning period and are therefore increasingly important to adult learners.

Tools are of special importance in neurobiological learning: They are both super-symbols and instruments of learning—tangible results of learning how to learn. While seemingly common to virtually all neurobiological learning, they are used differently by traumatic and transformational learners. One of the most obvious examples of this is in the way traumatic learners use the same tools, language for instance, to control and dominate—teach—others, while transformational learners focus on individual curiosity, exploration, and discovery—demonstration and mentorship.

As a result of using these steps, phases, or levels of learning and one's variously acquired tools, physical and functional changes take place in the neurobiological system. These changes in turn have profound ramifications with regard to other body organs and systems. An activated immune system, for example, will play a direct and aggressive role in physical de- and remyelination. Once again, neurobiological learning becomes intricately integrated into the body, mind, and spirit, and *vice versa*.

Normal neurophysical development creates distinctive learning periods. On the other hand, secondary growth in brain cell number, size, and extent, the establishment of replacement as well as new neural pathways, and myelin recrafting occur even after puberty, through the power of neurobiological learning.

The Sixth Law

Effective educators don't teach. Learners need to be free to identify and self-select the learning opportunities they need. Mentors need to concentrate on demonstrating transformative learning in their own lives, while at the same time recognizing, acknowledging, and working within individual-learner, rhythmic learning-cycle limitations.

Demonstration by application—unabashedly going through the frustration of prediscovery, acknowledging the power of error, and experiencing the joy of discovery alongside the learner—is mentor-assisted transformational learning at its finest!

An effective mentor supports any and all transformative learning, no matter how serendipitous. Transformational learning, because it is volitional, is always "right." Learners know, sometimes consciously, sometimes subconsciously at their developmental level, exactly what they need. They may not be able to verbalize these needs well, but they are quite capable of searching for and discovering them.

Classical teaching stresses the importance of such things as predefined course syllabi (the infamous "learning [business] contract" between teacher and learner) and curricula. During neurobiological learning, however, they are of little value. Similarly, concerns over "teaching" styles, strategies, and techniques become all but irrelevant. What is important is the diversity, richness, and immediate availability of learning resources—what many first-time observers to my classroom disdainfully call "clutter." I am occasionally asked, "How can anyone learn in all this clutter?" They do, and very effectively. Transformational learners and mentors acquainted with the neurobiological method often tell me aside, "What are they talking about? How can anyone learn anything in a place that's all 'hands off,' 'do not touch,' 'do not move'?" For my American Academic English class, I maintain a one-page combination syllabus and curriculum, alongside *ten volumes of aural and written resources*, instant learner access to online computers, and shelves of learning objects requested by learners. Ah, clutter.

Neurobiological learning is heavily object- rather than reason-, logic-, or plan-driven. In conventional teaching, the teacher must not only be the engine, conductor, engineer, waiter/waitress, entertainer, maintenance person, and cleanup crew, but also provide all train cars, clean, attractive, and arranged in the "correct" order and ready to move. Students have only to get on board and "ride the train" to a stated, predetermined destination. With neurobiological learning, the learner is the engine and engineer, the mentor a conductor. At some point the train, when assembled correctly by the learner, will begin moving to a destination often only apparent to the learner on arrival.

In traditional teaching, student questions always seem the same: "When do we arrive at the station?" For the neurobiological learner, the question is more like "When will the station arrive at the train?"

Neurobiological learning proceeds against a backdrop of developmental learning periods. Some, like adolescence, are, for teachers and parents, disturbingly active periods. Learning seems to occur only after lots of rhythmic physical activity, and then suddenly, in huge leaps, one after another. Others, like the much beloved latency period, resemble more closely a quiescent or resting period, during which learning seems slowly but constantly subject to neurobiological tweaking.

Teachers, at professional meetings, never cease their search for "tricks of the trade." Students seem to be forever waiting for something new and exciting from their teacher. Transformational mentors don't need a "bag of tricks," but they do need to be aware of not only the processes, but also the limits of neurobiological learning. Process-wise, with adequate mentoring and resources, transformational learners will generate their own excitement; quiet times become exactly that. In such situations, curiosity, discovery, and the thrill of learning will surface spontaneously when it's time.

Another neurobiological limitation I have observed in the classroom is that post-pubertal transformational learners seem able to tolerate a maximum of ten to fifteen minutes of continuous, focused, intensive object-data movement work. Afterward, they require a break. This particular neurobiological phenomenon is easily demonstrable.

Most learners I have encountered are not highly conscious of internal sensations—"feelings," or technically, kinesthesias—sometimes called biorhythms. An astute mentor can be of great assistance in developing an awareness of feelings, a felt sense of both their cyclic rhythm(s) and internal time consciousness. Most transformational learners I work with appear to tolerate "feeling" work for roughly thirty to sixty minutes. Again, afterward, learners require a break—usually a more substantial one than that required after intensive neurosensory object-data work.

Again, in my experience, most transformative learners seem to tolerate symbolic work for two to six hours at a time, but they then require even greater rest. After a period of intensive symbolic and interpretive work, I have frequently observed, both in therapy and in the classroom, what I consider to be the classical physical signs of neurophysiological integration and reintegration: yawning, muscle stretching, laughing, and joking. Often learners vocalize the need to "do something else," like daydream, rest, exercise, or even take a brief nap. After social-, world-, or spiritual-metacognitive-level learning, even deeper rest periods seem to occur in a roughly three- to twelve-hour cycle. As learning periods naturally lengthen, rest periods seem to become more individualistic.

In addition, a minimum amount of physiologically effective sleep seems absolutely necessary to avoid learning interference at any and all steps, phases, or levels. This appears necessary to allow routine hierarchical sorting and resorting, as well as remyelination, to proceed. I have heard this spoken of as creating the "mental space" necessary to allow ongoing neurobiological learning.

Of particular interest to me have been opportunities for effective learning that include or parallel lucid sleep, such as directed daydreaming, regression, and various forms of physically grounded play. There is some admittedly still sparse evidence that longer rhythms, cycles, or spirals of effective neurobiological learning may exist. I have often speculated whether such "supercognitive" steps, phases, or levels might involve archetypal or even mythical learning. It's intriguing to relate these as being related to the different, popularized "ages" of adult life—"Your young men shall dream dreams, and your old shall have visions."

In my experience, learners know what they need to learn, and they know the exact structure and pace they need to most successfully acquire it—it is we observers who have yet to catch up to them. The bumper-sticker message is clear: "Allow serendipity, drive your own car, and don't follow too close."

The Seventh Law

The neurobiological method underlies all teaching and learning method-ologies. Males and females develop different approaches to learning. Reasons, rules, meaning, sense, and truth are defined by the learner. When strongly "felt," what has been learned seems real or true, but their reality and truth-value are always open to reinterpretation.

Neurobiological learning occurs in today's classrooms, irrespective of the teaching methods employed. Some transformational learning seems to occur even in spite of teaching. It follows that NL *must* underlie other teaching methodologies. If this is so, then mentoring should prove consistently superior to teaching, even in the classroom. This is a powerful, testable prediction, coming directly from neurobiological theory and method.

According to the neurobiological evidence and theory, there are distinct differences in learning between males and females. There are, for example, observable differences in object interests between the sexes. These differences are of enormous importance to teachers, but of considerably lesser importance to mentors, as long as mentors "follow the lead" of learners. A more important issue for mentors would be whether same-sex mentor-learner pairings are more effective than opposite-sex pairings. I will hazard a guess that same-sex pairings will prove to be of greater importance for younger learners, opposite-sex pairings will prove of greater importance to adolescents, and adults will have diverse but highly individualistic needs, wants, and desires.

Humans, as a group, seem to me to have a learning capacity that is, as yet, nowhere near its zenith. Based on extrapolations from recent clinical and experimental studies, the human capacity for effective—hopefully transformational—learning, and thereby the power of the neurobiological theory and method, can be considered to be in its infancy. Human sentience, based on my work with self- and metacognition, is neither fully understood nor has it, when coupled with transformational learning, begun to show any sign of peaking yet. Our understanding of intelligence and cognition, for example, and its neurobiological development, according to these modified tenets, should prove applicable to fetuses and to other animals as well.

NEW STUDY, NEW LEARNING

I admit to being tired of reading about how the attention of disheartened, disinterested classroom students might be rekindled if only the teacher had something new—one more new trick up his or her sleeve, like a performer trying to play to a tired house. From a neurobiological point of view, most of these situations are the result of varying degrees of personal violation, and the "most effective" new tricks are simply more violating—much like movie sequels have to be more violent in order to simply capture the same attention. I wonder, instead of invoking traumatic learning, how easily these students' attentions could have been recaptured simply by introducing, for example, an oscillating object into their peripheral visual field. But that's just another trick. Isn't it?

Actually, no. It's a matter of using a "natural" neurological behavior inherent to all learners—much like a good dolphin trainer builds a show upon natural dolphin behaviors. From my own experience, this approach works. Better yet would be to introduce a peripheral learning object without invoking traumatic learning. But then such a limited approach would never have been needed if, in fact, the learning had been transformational in the first place. In the "real" teaching world, tired teachers and students struggle against the odds to acquire and retain what they must know to pass a test, and they end up traumatically learning much more than they needed, wanted, or desired.

One new, fashionable learning theory after another has promised to revive students, make teaching more effective and, in the end, make the business of education more profitable—and they always seem to use the same tried-and-true "teaching" methods and techniques that everyone is familiar with. One by one they invariably fail. Why? All, in one way or another, in order to be effective, invoke traumatic learning. All, in one way or another, are variations of the same thing: the efficient cloning and transfer of Platonic ideations from a teacher (controller, perpetrator) to a student (controllee, victim)—infinite variations of effective, traumatic learning. It's never been a problem of how to shovel more ideas into the brains of begrudging students. In the end, we don't learn most of the ideas anyway. What we learn and reinforce in such a system is the trauma.

I sincerely hope that we are on the threshold of letting go of 2000 years of violation. It is time to understand the neurobiological nature of traumatic learning—teaching—acknowledge our parts in it, and begin moving to transformational learning. The fact that trauma occurs so early in our lives and is so ubiquitous tends to obscure the common underlying neurobiological processes involved. Regardless of the weapon employed, violation inevitably invokes trauma, and trauma invokes traumatic learning. I am sharing with you, in this observation, one of the most unsettling shocks to my own system. For years I have watched, with sadness, "teachers" from every discipline "re-victimize" their students over and over and over again—and increasingly so with each repetition—through a combination of indifference, repression, denial, and repetition compulsion, though thankfully rarely with malice.

It's time to stop the ever-widening, institutionalized "circles of violence," let go of our stranglehold on teaching, and simply begin applying transformational learning. This is a charge for all of us—institutions, educators, teachers, staff, students, and parents alike—to at least try implementing transformational learning and mentorship.

Chapter Nine

A Great Theory . . . How's It Working?

LEARNING THE LINGO

What often happens to a new educational theory is that it gets polished up, shown off, and then . . . quickly retired to the academic library stacks. In 1998, while I was developing the neurobiological learning (NL) theory and method, a colleague I much respected, Mr. Joel Weaver, MA TESOL, the director of the Intercultural Communications College (ICC) in Honolulu, Hawaii, asked me to become a teacher there and to demonstrate transformational learning (TL) in the classroom. I never hesitated. If I could demonstrate TL in a real classroom, I was sure it could work pretty much everywhere. I pulled neurobiological learning off the academic shelf, dusted it off, and pressed it into service. After all, at some point I would have to put my money where my mouth was—as a "teacher" (we finally ended up calling ourselves "instructors" because "mentor" simply wasn't part of the school's administrative or professional vocabulary).

Looking back, it was a huge risk and quite possibly premature to move from clinically based theory so directly into the teaching classroom. Still, I had taught in universities for over thirty years and, well, I dearly loved education and wanted to see if I could help make it more effective and less traumatic. I loved my students (the term "learners" still hasn't completely caught on), and this was, after all, a reality-based venue within which to test NL theory and method, an excellent opportunity to apply transformational learning in a traditional teaching environment.

It is, of course, in the application of theory and method that some of the deepest and most profound secrets are revealed. In late 1999 I thought that NL theory and method, while it was in some respects still incomplete, stood poised and "ready enough" for application. By early 2000 my American Academic English program was fully implemented, this time incorporating transformational learning. Mostly.

Right from the start, the vast majority of students blossomed like wildflowers after a heavy rain. Bingo! Hooray! But a few didn't. Open student evaluations revealed that some students, particularly those who had become extraordinarily adept at learning *about* English—what many schools erroneously call traditional "grammar teaching"—had difficulty applying and using English in discovery. I'm not talking about very many—actually one or two out of eighty or so, roughly two percent. But they voiced their frustration loudly and openly, often to the point of demanding that they be allowed to return to a style of learning with which they were more comfortable, familiar, and adept.

Initially I worked exclusively with TL, applying it to a single English for Special Purposes (ESP) American Academic English class. It was nicknamed "TOEFL," after the Test of English as a Foreign Language (Educational Testing Service, Princeton, New Jersey), which most students in the class reluctantly need to conquer. After little more than a year, it became apparent from official TOEFL scores, college-acceptance ratios, and first-year university study completion rates that the program (and by implication, NL theory and TL) was a big winner. Course elections were up 1200 percent (!), monthly TOEFL scores increased an average of 300 percent, virtually all students were being accepted at American universities of *their* choice, and only one of over forty students who had gone on to study at an American college or university exited because of poor performance. Compare this with five disgruntled preprogram students with below international-average monthly TOEFL score increases, one in five students going on to *any* college or university at all, and a classic 75 percent failure rate for first-year university studies. Students, teachers, staff, and school owners were in agreement: Not bad for the "new boy on the block." Not bad at all!

That's the good news—and yet, almost immediately other teachers at the school raised an interesting question: Was this just a fluke? Maybe it was what seemed to many teachers my "eclectic" teaching style. If NL theory were "real," then TL should be able to be "taught" equally well by other instructors. Could I teach a classically trained "teacher" this new method? Would someone else trained in the theory and method be equally successful in the classroom? Would TL work equally well in a teaching venue other than "ESP, high-intermediate American Academic English"? Could such a radically different way of "teaching" be transferred successfully to another class within another school? After some discussion, I resolved to take on each of these challenges, one by one.

TEACHING THE TEACHERS

It proved more difficult than I had imagined to find a classical "teacher" who could successfully make the transition to "mentor." My first unsuccessful mentor-candidate was a seasoned teacher with a master's degree in teaching English as a second language (TESL) and an excellent command of American Academic English grammar. My second unsuccessful mentor-candidate was a recently graduated doctor of philosophy in linguistics from a top-rated, world-class institution. But it took a third mentor-candidate, Margaret Bills, an educator with a bachelor's degree in intercultural communication and limited English teaching experience, to successfully "catch" it. Even now, after several years of daily TL application experience, Maggie and I both still find ourselves slipping back every so often into "teaching" mode. Why is mentoring so difficult to acquire, and why is it so difficult to maintain?

Exit interviews were conducted with the two teachers who, in my opinion, did not make the transition. The first, struggling with personal, situational problems, found mentoring discomforting, as it accentuated these problems. The second never "saw" the distinction between teaching and mentoring—violational and volitional learning. Neither teacher had the benefit of observing and working with me—we talked extensively *about* NL and TL but didn't work together. At the time I didn't think it was necessary; after all, they were both experienced educators. After this wake-up call, the fourth mentor-candidate, Hisako Saito, who had recently completed a master's degree in teaching English as a second language, had the advantage of discussing, observing, and working side by side with me for several months, asking questions as they came up. So much for trying to teach mentoring—mentorship is better learned transformationally.

Soon after Ms. Bills and I began applying NL-based TL in our respective classrooms, another "obvious" truism became apparent: Mentors, especially teachers who wish to transition to mentors, require extensive mentoring *practice*. It's like a physician who, while smoking a cigarette, advises the patient firmly not to smoke. Mentoring is about *demonstrating*; neurobiological and transformational learning are about *doing*. Ms. Bills and I would agree that during the uncomfortable, prediscovery stage, the temptation to slip back into "teaching" mode becomes quite strong. It is difficult—no, *painfully* difficult—to demonstrate one's discomfiture. For me, I imagine it like suffering naked in front of everyone while they watch. Perhaps it is a traumatic echo from either my own birth event, my own traumatic experiences, or the traumatic world that surrounds our little "island in the [transformational learning] sun."

THE CLASSROOM CRUCIBLE

Anticipating the need for a more objective field evaluation (and also to accommodate the few students who demanded a more traditional teaching approach), we divided the American Academic English program vertically into two levels: TOEFL 1 and TOEFL 2. TOEFL 1, described as a beginner-level, "introductory" course, used traditional teachers, teaching, and a reconstructionist methodology familiar to international students who had studied English as a second language (ESL) outside the USA. TOEFL 2, billed as an intermediate-level, "foundation" course, utilized a mentor instead of a teacher to model and catalyze curiosity-based, discovery-driven transformational learning.

When compared side by side, the impact of the two different approaches was nothing less than profound, though interestingly, the impact on the thoughts and attitudes of students, teachers, and staff was even more profound. For example, perceived differences in "course style" became an immediate "hot topic" among students. The result was that a new type of learner, respected and valued schoolwide by teachers, peers, and staff from both inside and outside the program, began to emerge. TOEFL 2 learners, both individually and as a group, far exceeded course requirements, quickly but quietly developed a strong sense of individual ability and self-worth, held the program in high esteem, and, by their choice, changed from traditional "one-month students" to "three- to six-month learners." That TOEFL 2 would meet and far exceed academic as well as learner and stakeholder goals and objectives became immediately evident to everyone, *even the few remaining critics!*

Ultimately, both TOEFL 1 *and* TOEFL 2 monthly student-test scores increased, the latter on average threefold over expected monthly TOEFL score increases.

There quickly came to exist a certain competition between the two levels—between teachers and mentors, as well as students and learners. But most interesting was the fact that TOEFL 1 students, in spite of TOEFL test-score increases, still had trouble *applying* American Academic English and continued to find difficult the transition from teaching to mentorship, student to learner, traumatic to transformational learning. In fact, TOEFL 1 students moving to TOEFL 2 generally experience a brief drop in TOEFL score before "adjusting" and substantially increasing their monthly scores.

This appears true for "lower" as well as "higher" TOEFL 1 students. A few TOEFL 1 students, because of personal preferences, remained in TOEFL 1 until attaining scores roughly equivalent to "high" TOEFL 2 students. Nonetheless, upon transferring, the same transitory drop was noted, followed within about two to four weeks by "normally" accelerated TOEFL 2 scores.

It seemed to us that transitioning from traumatic to transformational learning was a shock to their systems. I don't fully understand this phenomenon even now. TOEFL 1 students who advanced to TOEFL 2 seemed to me to be awaiting being taught even while watching their TOEFL scores momentarily stop or fall. I recall overhearing two TOEFL 1 students saying, "Well, TOEFL 2 is OK if you *really* want to go to college or university." An interesting statement—did some American Academic English students really *not* want to go on to study at a college or university? Or was there more to this than what meets the eye?

THE FIRE WITHIN

The next year we decided to explore this phenomenon. New students and learners were asked to indicate whether they were primarily interested in an "academic" or a "college- or university-bound" track. Interestingly, most of the TOEFL 1 students indicated that they were college or university bound and remained so throughout the program. Most went on to attend local two-year community colleges. The rest generally transferred into TOEFL 2. About half the entering TOEFL 2 students, *including many TOEFL 1 transfers*, indicated academic interest only, but ninety percent changed to "college- or university-bound" before exiting! *Upon exit survey, we found that TOEFL 1 students were self-selecting for "lesser" or "easier" community-college training, while TOEFL 2 students (including TOEFL 1 graduates unsure of their ability to take on baccalaureate or graduate study) actually changed their self-image, goals, and expectations during their TOEFL 2 program work.* Clearly *something* special was happening in TOEFL 2.

Over the last year, both TOEFL 1 and 2 have become more parallel than serial, though it would be more correct to say that most TOEFL 1 students interested in baccalaureate or higher-level studies transition to TOEFL 2 and curiosity-based, discovery-driven, mentor-supported trans-formational learning. Most, but not all. A few, like our first two mentor-candidates, seem either unable or wary of making the transition. This is an area of considerable interest not only to myself and colleagues, but also to learners and staff both within and outside the program. If nothing else, TL has opened new avenues of inquiry, where in fact few existed be-fore. It is as if TOEFL 2 "awakens" most people who come into contact with it.

We are considering a double crossover study (unfortunately, not blind) to further explore differences between teaching and transformational learning-mentorship.

And as far as the business of education, since its second month the TOEFL 2 program has been and remains the predominate ESP program at ICC and a major financial success.

CURRICULUM—THE UNREAL THING

A topic of particular interest has been program curriculum development. ICC ·is a nationally accredited institution. During periodic accreditation reviews, curricula are subject to intense scrutiny and evaluation. Our TOEFL 2 course curriculum, although continuing to evolve, is unusual. For instance, our daily lesson plans, at first anticipatory discovery guides, have slowly evolved into a single-page syllabus-curriculum summary of learning resources.

The number and quality of resource materials, on the other hand, have exceeded and continue to exceed all predictions. As mentioned earlier, there are now a *TOEFL 2 Study Guide*; nine volumes of high-student-interest topic materials with over 400 interactive writing, reading, and listening opportunities; one online computer for each learner; and numerous boxes of items requested by learners at various times currently available to TOEFL 2 mentors and students.

As a result of what some ICC teachers identify as the "positive feel" of the program, several attempts have been made to incorporate select NL/TL tenets into traditionally taught classes. This has been especially so for teachers favoring a "learner-centered classroom" approach. While there are superficial similarities between this and the neurobiological/ transformational approach, the differences are profound. The "learner-centered classroom" is still a taught approach, subject to the liabilities of traumatic learning. What is needed is not just a change in *emphasis* from teacher to learner, but a more fundamental shift from traumatic teaching to transformational learning.

The ascendance of learning resources over classroom curriculum in transformational learning has prompted several within the TOEFL program to attempt to apply NL/TL theory and tenets within nontraditional teaching venues. For example, for a brief time we offered "TOEFL by Internet." We quickly learned that success with language acquisition over distance was dependent on the successful establishment of a worldwide network of trained or at least interested in-training mentors. Similarly, private tutors both within and outside the school have shown interest in applying NL and especially TL theory and tenets. Our experience with the application of NL/TL within these two special venues, we believe, indicates that NL/TL may provide the single workable, unified theoretical and methodological learning framework for classroom, tutoring, and distance learning that has been so historically elusive. My interest in this particular area has prompted me to write a sequel to this book addressing this specific issue.

These interesting characteristics of NL/TL are creating intriguing new areas for research by TOEFL program, school, and "outside" faculty. Interest grows steadily in establishing an international neurobiological learning discussion forum, neurobiological learning society, a neurobiological-transformational learning mentorship certification program, and an ongoing professional development program for mentors, each of which is in various stages of evolution as I write.

TRANSFORMING FAILURE

Mentorship invites an entirely new learning element, which I call *adhibition*—the use of student-selected topic and object learning resources to invite discovery and transformative learning. Adhibition is perhaps the first seed of an NL teaching pedagogy, if such a thing can be said to truly exist. Within our program, adhibition has begun evolving into a TOEFL Mentor Guide broadly addressing issues of training, preparation, experience, practices, and attitudes surrounding effective transformational mentorship. One area of particular interest has been turning teaching failure and "failures of discovery" into transformative learning experiences.

In the first case, it must be remembered that teaching failures—usually defined as instances in which the teacher is unable to "answer" one or more student questions—have little if anything to do with NL. They are, in fact, largely irrelevant, since mentors are not expected to "know all the answers," or to foist their own ideas and ideals onto their students. In this sense, NL often begins in the teaching classroom with teaching failures, *de facto* instances where a teacher is finally placed out of the way of learning. Let the learning begin!

Failures of discovery are another beast altogether. Both mentor and learner quickly realize that they must "let go" of trying to control the popping-up or -out phenomenon—the very heart of discovery—and must instead focus their joint energies on the exploration process, following wherever it leads. But what if the exploration leads nowhere? What if no discoveries are made? What if . . . What if . . . What if . . . ?

While these are often excruciating concerns for teachers and "new" mentors, the answer is that it simply doesn't happen. The "problem" is actually with point of view: It's the difference between teaching a truth and learning a truth neurobiologically. "What if it doesn't happen?" is a legitimate teaching question, but like failures of teaching, it has little meaning in neurobiological terms. The mind is made to seek *and find* answers—to record, associate, symbolize, and interpret them, and to assign meaning to everything we sense. If there is one "innately, preprogrammed force" within the human mind, it is insatiable curiosity—"learning drive"—unless, of course, that curiosity or drive has been traumatically crushed. Even then, the drive to learn is so strong that when traumatic dams are broken, curiosity once again flows freely, exploding in any and every direction.

What *feels* like the anxiety of no discovery is actually prediscovery discomfort. Something must be abandoned to gain space for new insights. Tearing apart learned expectations evokes anxiety and even fear. Yet that's all it is: emotions and feelings. The best mentors openly acknowledge these emotions and feelings, relegate them clearly to prediscovery discomfort, and "hold the fort"—keep seeking—until the pop-up or -out phenomenon occurs and awakens discovery.

THE NEW YARDSTICK

During my explorations of NL in the classroom, I have come to the conclusion that there may actually be a second form of transformative learning. I have taken to calling this offshoot "disquisition," for lack of a better term. By disquisition, I mean seeking meaning through focused co-inquiry, analysis, and discussion of neurosensory phenomena—a process sometimes referred to by academicians as hermeneutic or interpretive inquiry.

Disquisitional learning has generated considerable interest from teachers of subsequent languages, who see in it a way of bridging international English-subsequent-language learners into independent, postsecondary learners, capable of competing successfully with native-speaking Americans in American colleges and universities.

Research into the neurobiological foundations of disquisitional learning, and its relationship to transformational learning and mentorship, have been going on in earnest for several years now at ICC. One result was, in fact, the "TOEFL by Internet" program. Another has been the development and successful implementation of "TOEFL 3," an advanced-level, disquisitional learning program in which ICC mentors, in partnership with college and university professors, develop, analyze, explain, and assist in the delivery of asynchronous, independent-study, distance-learning courses at ICC. The TOEFL 3 program disquisitional learning (DL) process has been so successful that several of us believe it to be the "answer" to successful, neurobiologically based, transformational distance learning.

LEARNING TO LEARN

Discovery-based transformative learning appears to favor individual, pair, and small-group work in a resource-rich environment, rather than in traditional classrooms or large lecture halls. Interestingly, the continued expansion of the Internet and World Wide Web present unique challenges to traditional teaching. They represent the beginnings of a "world library" encompassing the sum total of information, and they are one—though not the only—answer to creating an affordable, resource-rich TL or DL environment.

TL enjoys a noisy, "scramble"-style environment, anathema to traditional classroom teaching. In the course of developing ICC's TOEFL program, I have noted differences in the quality, quantity, and effectiveness of discovery, transformational, and disquisitional learning conducted among individuals, pairs, and small groups. Collectively, these observations are fostering an intensive reexamination of the definition, nature, and role of the "basic learning unit." For example, discussions have begun among TOEFL 2 faculty about how to marry peripatetic, open-field, exploratorium, Socratic, Montessori, correspondence, interactive-computer-assisted and asynchronous distance learning into neurobiologically based learning units that would catalyze discovery and transformative learning as well as make the move from teaching to mentorship smoother, less traumatic, and more efficient.

FUN AND GAMES

During program implementation, another characteristic of transformational learning that endears transformative learning to both new and continued learners is both child and adult play. We are still awakening to the central role of play in curiosity-based, discovery-driven, mentor-assisted, transformative learning (the Root-Bernsteins devote an entire chapter in their book to this topic).

Having had the distinct pleasure of repeatedly observing the discovery process in action, it seems to me that play has a most important role in the prediscovery process, somehow making the discomfort, anxiety, and occasional agony of this period not just tolerable, but exciting—to the point of compulsion! I suspect that herein lies the very essence of nontraumatic effective learning.

We are only now beginning to recognize, appreciate, and investigate play. For example, I recently began looking at the basic nature and desired form, if any, for "testing" within transformative learning. Could it, structured correctly, become a form of curiosity-based play? Interactive computer games are an example of curiosity-based play that, with proper computer algorithms, might be used for evaluation ("testing" by its very nature is traumatic) and perhaps even individual progress as well as augmenting mentorship (or possibly even replacing it over distance) within a transformational learning framework. Even preliminary work in this area has been wildly productive: For example, we found this area of interest to lead us to challenge and clarify the meaning of *learning authenticity* within transformational and disquisitional learning, and use Delphian capstone projects instead of tests.

RITUAL REVISITED

My clinical work with trauma survivors helped me recognize that the role of ritual in learning is still not fully realized, understood, or appreciated. Ritual is an important element in traumatic, neurobiologically based learning and, by implication, transformative and disquisitional learning. Our work at ICC with transformational learning within the TOEFL 2 course is bringing to light the singular importance of the capstone project as well as pre- and post-discovery preparatory and completion celebrations.

The former resulted in the development of special challenges with tangible rewards during each of the three, approximately one-month TOEFL 2 "terms" emphasizing writing, reading, and listening, respectively. For example, during writing block, learners self-select their "best" American expository essay and, with the assistance of a peer editor, create a journal that they publish and distribute. We estimate any recent issue of the ICC *Journal*—printed and Internet versions combined—may be read by over 10,000 people! As a further result, ICC's TOEFL 2 students can cite an expository essay they have written in American Academic English and have had published in a peer-reviewed journal when they apply to American colleges and universities.

During reading block, learners may elect to read a prominent American short story, and when they eventually discover the best answers to nine or more of ten multiple-choice, multiple-answer questions, they are rewarded by public recognition and the receipt of a gift certificate to purchase a book, written in American English, of their own (the Perfect Reader capstone).

Similarly, during listening block, learners may accept the challenge to view (as many times as they wish) a prominent American movie, and upon discovering the best answers to the same style of ten questions, are publicly given two "free" tickets to a local cinema to view a movie in American English, with a friend of their choice (the Picture Perfect capstone). These capstone challenges are eagerly accepted by most learners and, I find, are yet another profound discovery resource.

More recently, we have introduced the use of formal academic regalia by TOEFL 2 mentors at "graduation" (graduation automatically occurs when learners complete their studies or individually allotted time for study). I am quite interested in the role that anticipatory post-course recognition and academic "passing-through" rituals play in the transformative and disquisitional learning processes.

There is a tangible, growing realization among all ICC faculty members that capstone projects, pre- and post-discovery and completion rituals, may provide a platform for learners to discover, experience, and eventually "own" the transformative learning process for *themselves,* thus facilitating its continued use outside the initial learner-mentor and institutional environment. All in all, this is yet another example of how the application of neurobiological theory and method in transformative learning seems to catalyze discoveries not only in learners, but in mentors and virtually anyone else touched by the resulting program, including new research into the theory, method, and application itself—an indication, I believe, of the heuristic richness and primacy of both NL and transformative learning.

TRANSFORMATIVE LEARNING
IN A TRAUMATIC, TEACHING WORLD

In late 2002 I was challenged by school administrators to demonstrate the feasibility of formally training and certifying teachers in neurobiological learning theory and methodology, transformative learning, and disquisitional learning. Thus far one mentor-candidate has successfully negotiated the transition from teaching to mentorship to my satisfaction, including demonstrating recognition of traumatic learning, initiation and maintenance of mentorship, and the application of transformational teaching in the classroom. Currently, a second mentor-candidate, a former learner in the program who recently completed a master's degree in teaching English as a second language, is attempting the transition from teacher to mentor.

As I mentioned earlier, not everyone can do it. Successful transition clearly requires a working understanding of not only the neurobiology involved, but also the ability to attain and maintain mentorship and foster transformative learning in an otherwise traumatic world. It's a big challenge, but one with immense, tangible personal rewards to the successful. The world of education looks (and is) entirely different through neurobiological glasses.

Yet despite the challenges, interest in transformational learning continues to skyrocket. It is in response to this rapidly expanding interest that I wrote the first, much more detailed book, *A Neurobiological Theory and Method of Language Acquisition*, which although focusing on language acquisition, contains a much more comprehensive development and explanation of the neurobiological learning theory and method. I heartily commend it to readers of this book with a professional interest in neurobiological and transformative learning. I am working as I write this second book, to establish neurobiological, transformational, and disquisitional learning certificates based on a combination of unit mastery reading of the first and this second book, along with a directed mentorship experience either with myself, with a trained TOEFL 2 mentor at ICC, or by distance through association with a certified regional mentor (CRM) at or near the mentor-candidate's work site.

By popular request, I have established both an Internet-based NL resource web page at http://www.freewebs.com/neurobiological/index.htm

and an NL discussion forum at http://www.internetstitute.com/cgi-bin/ forum/YaBB.cgi/YaBB.cgi?board=3 for educators, teachers, tutors, distance educators, mentors, linguists, psychologists, counselors, learners, and parents. The vicissitudes of the Internet being what they are, I will try to maintain these resources for those interested in NL, TL, and DL as long as possible—if by the time you read this book these links are no longer active, then please try an Internet search specifying "Janik, neurobiological" or e-mail me at djanik@icchawaii.edu, where I will always be pleased to hear from you. I am especially interested in any observations you may have regarding the application of NL, TL, or DL theory or tenets in your own situation.

I also mentioned a Neurobiological Learning Society currently on the Internet at http://drjanik.tripod.com/nls.html. The society is already generating public, institutional, and general academic interest. But that's another story in development. If you or your institution are interested in this effort, please e-mail me. Neurobiological, transformational, and disquisitional learning are already becoming, in a word, "exceptionally" hot topics.

Chapter Ten

A Personal Invitation

Even today, teacher training rarely includes neurobiology, or neurobiological, transformative or disquisitional learning. I suspect this is because most academic educators and teacher-trainers are themselves largely unfamiliar with what is now known clinically, experimentally, and through medical-imaging studies of the physical structure and function of the body. In addition, I am not aware of any other intact neurobiological learning theories or methodologies that have been derived from the vast storehouse of clinical knowledge and experience that exists regarding "effective" teaching and learning—trauma—and its equally effective therapeutic reflection, curiosity-based, discovery-driven, mentor-assisted transformational learning.

As a result, neurobiological and transformational theories and methods have been slow to be assimilated, even by interested teachers. Still, clinical, experimental, and imaging reports that impact our understanding of neurobiological and transformational learning continue to appear in the literature and are slowly but steadily continuing to develop what I have called the "new" German school of biologically based learning and linguistics—neurobiological learning (NL), for short. Through the contributions of these pioneers, the tradition remains alive and, despite its obscurity to most teachers, is now rapidly coming of age. To this august tradition, I add my own, distinctly clinical and linguistic, perspective. I have tried to correlate contemporary clinical data with contemporary experimental and imaging data, reformulating these often scattered, yet closely interrelated, pieces into a single cohesive neurobiological theory of learning, replete with method and tenets. From this I have attempted to derive a theory and method of effective, nontraumatic, transformational learning. Last, I have

summarized some of my most important observations and thoughts that
have arisen as a result of the application of these theories and methodologies in the classroom at ICC.

I have no illusions that this book will answer all your questions about
NL, TL, or DL. Nor will it answer many of the specific teaching questions
I am commonly asked. How should an optimized TL-based classroom and
school be constructed? Exactly how much time should be allocated to
oral, aural, and written work? NL, TL, and DL are, after all, not about
teaching, classrooms, and schools—the business of teaching—but rather
about letting and encouraging effective learning to occur in learners. This
is not just a semantic argument—it is a fundamental shift in education
that, as I have tried to show, has profound ramifications. It is not a better
teaching world—it is a new learning world altogether.

That this neurobiological theory will eventually prove to be the long-
sought-after unifying theory underlying all effective educational as well
as traditional classroom teaching theories and methods is, of course, my
hope. That it will, at the least, command attention and inspire each of you
to critically examine current, mostly ideationally based theories and methods of teaching, and continue the development of NL, TL, and DL theory
and methodology, is my sincere desire.

The neurobiological theory and method, especially transformational
learning, with its emphasis on learning, mentorship, curiosity, discovery,
and transformation as applied at Intercultural Communications College,
continues to boldly produce rich, new, testable hypotheses and insights
into the nature of education, learning, and both first and subsequent language acquisition. Equally important, these insights are already opening
up new, promising areas of research. The genie is now out of the bottle.
Wishes have been made. Education is now being freed from the tyranny
of traumatic teaching, and the world around us has begun to change.

As NL, TL, and DL theory and methodology are explored, applied,
tested, and evaluated here and elsewhere, an increased understanding of
the basic tenets, underlying mechanisms, possible further applications, and
ultimate educational potential will follow, as sure as day follows night. I
believe that it is time to let go of the trappings of rhetorical and ideational
methodologies, and of our grip on direct proof. A learning theory and methodology grounded solidly in anatomy, physiology, and biochemistry, incorporating the wealth of contemporary clinical, experimental, and imag-

ing data available, forged in the heat of indirect (scientific) proof, and applicable to the broadest range of learning environments—not just in the traditional "teaching classroom"—now exists. It is true that neurobiological and transformational learning requires teachers to assimilate a massive and furiously growing body of physical data as well as to rethink some of the most fundamental precepts of teaching and learning. The evidence indicates that such efforts are well justified and will be generously rewarded.

Neurobiological and transformational learning theory and method present a unique opportunity for educators and linguists to retake control of a profession that has lingered long enough in the Dark Ages and bring it into the light of mainstream scientific inquiry.

I would like to personally invite you, the next generation of neurobiological and transformational learning pioneers, to *take charge of humanity's out-of-control traumatic learning process, turn it about, and jumpstart it on the path to neurobiologically based, transformational learning. The rewards—knowledge, wisdom, and profound enlightenment grounded in physical reality—are there for the taking.*

References

Brazil: Nunca Mais. (1985). Petropolis: Vozes.

Dassin, J. (Ed.). (1986). *Torture in Brazil* (English translation by James Wright). New York: Vantage Books.

Deacon, T. (1997). *The Symbolic Species*. New York: W. W. Norton.

Freud, S. (2000). *The Standard Edition of the Complete Psychological Works of Sigmund Freud* (Ed. J. Strachey). New York: W. W. Norton. [Note: Difficult reading? Yes, but though everyone knows and even quotes Freud liberally, how many people do you know who have actually read his works?]

Gopnik, A., Meltzoff, A., & Kuhl, P. (1999). *The Scientist in the Crib*. New York: William Morrow.

Gray, P. The Assault on Freud. *Time* (1993, November 29), 142(23), 47–51.

Irwin, J. (1973). *To Rule the Night: The Discovery Voyage of Astronaut Jim Irwin*. Philadelphia: A. J. Holman.

Janik, D. (2004). *A Neurobiological Theory and Method of Language Acquisition*. Munich: Lincom Europa.

Kessler, R. (2000). *The Soul of Education*. Alexandria: Association for Supervision and Curriculum Development.

Lenneberg, E. (Ed.). (1964). *New Directions in the Study of Language*. Cambridge: MIT Press.

Lenneberg, E., & Lenneberg, E. (Eds.). (1975). *Foundations of Language Development, Volumes 1 and 2*. New York: Academic Press.

Lorenz, K. (1943). *Die angeborener Formen möglicher Erfahrung* [English: Innate forms of possible experience]. *Zeitschrift für tierpsychologie*, (5)2, 235–409. [Note: There are numerous "free" online services that can translate this interesting article from German into English, if you would like to read it for yourself.]

McGuinness, D. (1985). *When Children Don't Learn*. New York: Basic Books.

Milgram, S. (1983). *Obedience to Authority: An Experimental View*. New York: Harper/Collins.

Montessori, M. (1966). *The Secret of Childhood*. New York: Ballantine.

Pavlov, I. (2001). *I. P. Pavlov: Selected Works* (Ed. K. Koshtoyants). Honolulu: University Press of the Pacific.

Piaget, J. (1955). *The Language and Thought of the Child*. New York: Meridian.

Piaget, J. (1990). *Child's Conception of the World*. New York: Littlefield Adams.

Piaget, J. (2000). *The Psychology of the Child*. New York: Basic Books.

Root-Bernstein, R., & Root-Bernstein, M. (1999). *Sparks of Genius*. New York: Mifflin.

Snow, C. (1998). *The Two Cultures*. Cambridge: Cambridge University Press.

Spearman, C. (1923). *The Nature of "Intelligence" and the Principles of Cognition*. London: MacMillan.

Spearman, C. (1927). *The Abilities of Man: Their Nature and Measurement*. New York: MacMillan.

Sylwester, R. (1995). *A Celebration of Neurons*. Alexandria: Association for Supervision and Curriculum Development.

Sylwester, R. (2000). *A Biological Brain in a Cultural Classroom*. Thousand Oaks: Corwin Press.

van der Kolk, B. (1987). *Psychological Trauma*. Washington, DC: American Psychiatric Press.

Vernadsky, V. (1986). *Biosphere*. San Francisco: Synergistic Press.

Watson, J., & Rayner, R. (1920). Conditioned Emotional Reactions. *Journal of Experimental Psychology*, 3(1), 1–14.

Werner, E. (1971). *The Children of Kauai*. Honolulu: University of Hawaii Press.

Werner, E., & Smith, R. (1997). *Kauai's Children Come of Age*. Honolulu: University of Hawaii Press.

Werner, E. (1992). The children of Kauai: Resiliency and recovery in adolescence and adulthood. *Journal of Adolescent Health* (June 13), 262–268.

Weschler, L. (1998). *A Miracle, a Universe*. New York: Pantheon.

Zimbardo, P. (2004). *The Stanford Prison Experiment: A Simulation of the Psychology of Imprisonment Conducted at Stanford University*. Retrieved Sept 24, 2004, from http://www.prisonexp.org/. [Note: The experiment was funded by the Office of Naval Research. The original report by Haney, Banks, and Zimbardo in the *Office of Naval Research News* is quite difficult to access, so I offer instead Dr. Zimbardo's website, which includes one of the most authoritative reports on the experiment.]

Index

Index

About the Author

Daniel Janik is originally from Chicago, Illinois, America's heartland. Raised in Alaska, the last frontier, he received a BA from the University of Washington, a masters in public health from the University of California–Berkeley, an MD from Loma Linda University School of Medicine in California, and a PhD in education and linguistics from Bircham International University in Madrid, Spain. Dr. Janik is an honored fellow of the American College of Preventive Medicine and the American Association of Integrative Medicine. He lives in Honolulu, Hawaii, with his wife, Setsuko Tsuchiya, a licensed massage therapist, and serves as coordinator of American academic English programs at the Intercultural Communications College, a private English as a second language and American college/university preparatory school. He is the author of numerous publications, including *A Neurobiological Theory and Method of Language Acquisition* (2004).